THE WATER AND WOOD SHASTRAS

The Third Gungthang Rinpoche,
Venerable Konchok Tenpai Dronme

Translated by Yeshe Khedrup
and Wilson Hurley

Edited by Scott Bramlett and Casey Kemp

T0160073

KARUNA PUBLICATIONS

Published in 2012 by Karuna Publications
An Imprint of Diamond Cutter Press, LLC
55 Powderhorn Drive
Wayne, NJ 07470

All photos, illustrations and images are courtesy of Shutterstock
Images, LLC, except for the photo on page 110, which is courtesy of
CHEN WS / Shutterstock.com.

Printed in the United States

Book design by Clare Cerullo

Library of Congress Cataloging-in-Publication Data is available upon
request.

ISBN 978-0-9765469-9-3

www.karunapublications.org

THE WATER AND WOOD SHASTRAS

Contents

Editors' Notes

It is hoped that this brief overview will allude to the depth and profundity of Gungthang Rinpoche's poems. Their message is deep and vast, but deceptively simplified and presented beautifully through the metaphors of Gungthang Rinpoche's elegant verse.

We have provided endnotes, which include some selected comments on the text by Akya Yongdzin Yangchen Gawai Lodro (*A kya yongs 'dzin dbyangs can dga' ba'i blo gros*, 1740-1827). His endnotes constitute the only Tibetan commentary found thus far on the Water and Wood Shastras. They often help to shed light on some of the poems' more obscure references. Occasionally, we have added our own comments to Akya Yongdzin's, in which case brackets have been used. We have also omitted his comments pertaining exclusively to word definitions in order to reduce the number of endnotes, but we have considered them in our choice of wording for the translations.

Translators' Introduction

It is with great joy that we present these poems written by one of Tibet's greatest scholars and practitioners, Gungthang Tenpai Dronme.[1] Gungthang Rinpoche, as he is popularly known, composed these exquisite works in eighteenth century Tibet, which at the time was a culture largely concerned with harmony and maintaining balance with the natural world. These poems embody the central passion of Tibetan Buddhist culture—the pursuit of knowledge and compassion in order to actualize the highest potential of the human spirit.

These poems are unique in speaking to both secular and spiritual audiences. They are cherished among Tibetans due to their beauty, depth, and skill in presentation. Gungthang Rinpoche had an uncanny ability to speak to the hearts and minds of his time with profound messages made easy to comprehend. Like all great thinkers, the truths he elucidates transcend his own era and are still relevant and often quoted today. In the troubled waters of our current world situation, they are a breath of sanity drawn from ancient wisdom.

In Tibetan, poetry in general is called *nyengak*, which means "eloquent speech." Poetry was traditionally one of the "five minor sciences" studied in Tibet alongside the rules of meter, synonyms and antonyms, linguistics and drama.[2] In Sanskrit, eloquent speech was called *Subhasita* ("well-spoken words"). The Buddha, Siddartha Gautama (563 BCE to about 483 BCE) described four qualities of such speech in the *Subhasita Sutta*:

> *What is well-spoken, the good say, is foremost;*
> *Second, speak Dhamma, not non-Dhamma;[3]*
> *Third, speak what is pleasant, not unpleasant;*
> *Fourth, speak the truth, not falsehood.[4]*

The Buddha's disciple, Vangisa, elaborated on this by saying, "*One should utter only such speech by which one does not afflict oneself nor cause harm to others...speech that is gladly welcomed...brings them nothing evil...truth, indeed, is deathless speech...the secure speech which the Buddha utters for the attainment of Nibbana, for making an end to suffering, is truly the foremost speech.*"[5]

The *Subhasita* genre of literature flourished in ancient India. Nagarjuna, the founder of the profound lineage of the Middle Way, who lived in India around the second century C.E., wrote an example of such verse with his *The Staff of Wisdom* (Sanskrit: *Prajñadanda*). One verse from

Nagarjuna's poem reads:

> *Those who speak with discretion*
> *Are respected by mankind,*
> *As the sun, emerging from the shadows,*
> *By its rays creates great warmth.*[6]

The *Subhasita* tradition was also eventually taken up in Tibet by Sakya Pandita Kunga Gyaltsen (1182-1251) with his *Precious Treasury of Well-Spoken Advice* (Tibetan: *legs bshad rin po che'i gter*).[7] The latter's influence is mentioned near the end of the Wood Shastra where Gungthang Rinpoche writes:

> *By the jeweled lasso of whose fame,*
> *The edges of the earth of India and Tibet are tied,*
> *Glorious Sakya Pandita, I have relied*
> *On your path of well-spoken advice.*

In addition to their strength as examples of Subhasita literature, Gungthang Rinpoche's poems serve as *Shastras*. *Shastras* (Tibetan: *bstan bcos*) are commentaries on the Buddha's teachings meant to help transform the mind and protect it from negative states, which lead to suffering. The poems included in this volume use images from the natural world to illustrate profound insights into the nature of humanity and the path to enlightenment. The author draws upon his own experience of years of intensive spiritual study and meditation practice in order to articulate his realizations for the benefit of others.

It is hoped that the sheer beauty of Gungthang Rinpoche's verses will captivate the heart and give hours of joyful reading. The depth of meaning conveyed in these verses is profound and the eloquence with which he expresses himself is truly inspired. His rich imagery, drawn from water, from wood, and from ancient Indian Vedic mythology, both evokes emotion and arouses the intellect. No doubt, this literary work is an invaluable gem and its translation has been long overdue.

Biography of
Gungthang Tenpai Dronme

The third incarnation in the Gungthang line,[8] Gungthang Tenpai Dronme, was born in the lower Dzogey (*mdzod dge*) region of Amdo (Northeastern Tibet) in the Water Horse Year of the thirteenth Rabjung[9] (1762). His father was Chakpo Jam (*lcags po byams*) and his mother was Bochok (*bo cok*). From the time of his early childhood, unlike other children his age, he possessed astute wisdom and excellent manners. When he reached the age of five, a search party came looking for the reincarnation of the supreme emanation of Gungthang, and made an unerring recognition. Jamyang Shepa Rinpoche, Jikme Wangpo,[10] recognized him, determining that he was indeed the precious emanation of Gungthang.

At the age of seven, in the Earth Mouse year (1768), Gungthang Rinpoche was brought to Tashi Kyil monastery (*bkra shis 'khyil*) where he received both novice (*rab byung*) and apprentice (*dge thsul*) monastic vows at the same time from Jamyang Shepa Jikme Wangpo. He was given the name of Konchok Tenpai Dronme. For five years, he studied reading and writing with his teacher, Geshe Losang Rinchen (*dge ba'i bshes gnyen blo bzang rin chen*) and memorized topics on Dharma[11] practice along with the root texts of the Five Great Treatises.[12] During breaks, he listened to many Dharma lineage teachings of the Sutras and Tantras[13] from Jamyang Shepa Rinpoche.

In the Earth Dog year (1778) at the age of 17, wishing to continue his studies, he traveled to central Tibet and joined the Gomang monastic college of Drepung (*'bras spungs sgo mang gra tshang*). There he listened and studied, beginning with the initial scripture of the Perfection of Wisdom class, from his teacher, the great scholar and master, Hor Kelsang Ngodrup (*hor skal bzang dngos grub*). Over the course of nine years, he studied this and the first four of the Five Great Scriptures, becoming a worthy example for all great teachers.

When he was 21, in the Water Tiger year (1782), he received full Bhikshu[14] vows from the Eighth Dalai Lama, Jampel Gyatso (*ta' la'i bla ma sku phreng brgyad pa 'jam dpal rgya mtsho*), learning perfectly the practices and restrictions of what to safeguard and what to refrain from over the course of his life. This entailed studying the fifth of the Five Great Treatises (the *Vinaya*). He took the precious tutor of the Eighth Dalai Lama, Yeshe Gyaltsen (*ye shes rgyal mtshan*) and Longdol Lama Rinpoche (*klong rdol bla ma rin po che*) as his main teachers, and from them, listened to many Sutra and Tantra Dharma teachings that he had not previously heard.

At the age of 25, in the Fire Horse year (1786), he performed without compare for the title of Geshe Lharampa (*dge bshes lha rams pa*)[15] during examinations at the Great Monlam festival in Lhasa. Then, not long after, he returned to Amdo together with Jamyang Shepa Rinpoche. Over several years, he mainly pursued meditation, while simultaneously gathering many faithful disciples. He fulfilled each one's wishes and aspirations with extensive, vast teachings on Dharma lineages from Sutra and Tantra.

Jamyang Shepa Rinpoche passed way in 1791, so at the age of 31 during the Water Mouse year (1792), following requests from the leading house at Tashi Kyil monastery (*blab rang dpon tshang*, Jamyang Shepa's house) and supplications from the general body of monks, Gungthang Rinpoche became the great assembly's throne holder (Abbot). Over the next seven years, he rejuvenated traditional and special streams of Dharma through teaching, listening and studying. He used whatever skillful means were fitting in terms of rewards and consequences in order to re-establish the regulations, rules and so forth. Thus, he renewed whatever had degenerated or had been lost by making serious efforts towards activities promoting and increasing what little remained. Because of this, compared to before, the number of monks, the extent of their studies, and their patronage were all greatly enhanced and increased.

When Gungthang Rinpoche was 37, in the Earth Mouse year (1798), the supreme emanation of his teacher—Jamyang Shepa Rinpoche's reincarnation—Jikme Gyatso (*jigs med rgya mtsho*), was established on the monastery's throne. Afterwards, Gungthang Rinpoche stepped down from his responsibilities as the great assembly's throne holder. Then, for several years, he held the responsibilities of the throne for Gonlung monastery (*dgon lung gi thri khur*).

When he was 42, during the Water Pig year (1802), he began the construction of a precious, new Stupa[16] granting liberation on sight. He completed it when he was 44, in the Wood Ox year (1805) and held a consecration celebration. Moreover, people from many places including Dzoge (*mdzod dge*), Chone (*co ne*), Gyelrong (*rgyal rong*), and Ngapa (*rnga pa*) invited him to come. So he traveled and taught, promoting many Dharma streams of Sutra and Tantra, enhancing studies at the monasteries, restoring degenerated rules and regulations, mediating regional conflicts and disputes, and helping people to refrain from killing birds, wild animals, fish and so forth. In these and other ways, he performed many great activities for the benefit of beings.

Countless disciples, great beings holding the Dharma, and holy ones arose because of his skillful means.

As for his compositions, he wrote *Comments on the Interpretable and the Definitive, A Detailed Analysis of the Basis of All, A Thorough Explanation of the Four Truths, A Detailed Analysis of Dependent Origination,*[17] and other texts cutting through the difficult points of the great scriptures. He also wrote many texts like *Praise and Commentary on Kurukulli,*[18] concerning Secret Mantra. Further compositions include *The Meaningful—an Auto-Commentary to the Praise of the Supreme Guru, The Water and Wood Shastras, A Discourse on Old Age and Youth, The Biography of Jamyang Shepa Jikme Wangpo, The Throne-Holder Losang Dondrup's Life Story, The Biography of Tuuken Chokyi Nyima,* and *The Life Story of Gomang's Abbot Chodar* .[19]

In all, his collected works comprise eight volumes, of which there are wood blocks in both Lhasa and Tashi Kyil. Most exceptionally, they contain numerous gems of uplifting advice benefiting the best, middling and least of mental aptitudes. Therefore, throughout the Central, Western, Kam and Amdo regions of Tibet, every top scholar in a single voice called him Gungthang Jampelyang (*gung thang 'jam dpal dbyangs*)[20] in order to praise him.

At the age of 62, in the Water Sheep year of the 14th Rabjung (1823), he passed away with the intent to benefit others. Some amazing relics were found in the ashes from his cremation, which were enshrined in a stupa. Pelsang Konchok Gyeltsen (*dpal sang dkon mchog rgyal mthsan*) wrote an extensive biography of his life entitled *The Sun Opening Faith's Lotus—the Life Story of Konchok Tenpai Dronme, Manjushri, Holder of the Great System of the Victor*.[21] It was included in the eighth volume of that holy one's collected works (volume *nya*), numbering 194 pages, and can be found at Lhasa Sholparma.[22]

The Two Subjects of the Water and Wood Shastras

Gungthang Rinpoche divides the subject matter of both the Water and the Wood Shastras into two distinct sections. In the Water Shastra he begins with verses aimed at secular ethics and ends with a section on the stages of the path to enlightenment. The content of the first section serves as a basis for the last. Gungthang Rinpoche states:

> *How can the person unable to ford a stream*
> *Swim the ocean?*
> *How can the person who does not understand basic decency*
> *Comprehend the system of the Dharma?*[23]

In the Wood Shastra, he reverses the order, beginning with an overview of the path to enlightenment and ending with a section on secular ethics. He points out how the former approach benefits even our worldly interests with the verse:

> *If a tree's fruit is well nurtured,*
> *Leaves, branches and such will come by the way.*

If you make efforts in the holy Dharma,
By that, worldly glory will also be achieved.[24]

The path of Dharma naturally leads to approaching our lives in a noble manner. It is the key for building a decent society and a safe world in which to live. In any case, it might be appropriate to discuss the relevance of both topics for modern day living.

Secular Ethics

One only has to keep current with the news to be aware of the tragedies caused by human failings. Murder, terrorism, corruption, exploitation, and environmental devastation are all effects of human actions based on thoughts of hatred, greed, narcissism and other afflictions of the mind. Religions traditionally promote ethics and human decency, but we can see instances in which religious doctrine is used as justification for inhumane acts of violence, intolerance and cruelty. Even those who try to follow their religion well have to interact with people from various belief systems who may or may not concur with what constitutes decent behavior. Also, many others do not seem to have a serious interest in religious thought or are even opposed to it.

Therefore, secular ethics are indispensable for all of us to co-exist in human society. As soon as a system of ethics is identified as belonging to a particular school of religious thought, those who do not adhere to that particular religion may feel no obligation to live by it. Those with no religious beliefs may also feel uncompelled. Societal laws fill in this gap to a degree, but are also often disregarded by large segments of society.

Gungthang Rinpoche's verses on secular ethics (verses 5 through 79 of the Water Shastra and verses 36 through 100 of the Wood Shastra) are therefore a valuable resource for growing efforts by decent people everywhere to find common ground. He uses metaphor and irony to expose indecent behavior and to illustrate the inherent weakness of a corrupt lifestyle. He also offers compelling arguments for developing an ethical approach to life. In addition, he illustrates how societies stand or fall based on the characters of both their leaders and citizens.

Fundamentals of the Path of Dharma

Gungthang Rinpoche's verses on Buddhist Dharma follow the format of *Lamrim*, the graded stages on the path to enlightenment. It is difficult to follow the logic of the stages of the path unless one has a working knowledge of the basic principles of Buddhism. First and foremost, it is important to understand a Buddhist view of birth, life and death.

We know we were born, that we are currently alive, and that we will die at some point, but the rest remains unclear. In the West, there are two opposing views about life and death that seem to predominate: theism verses scientific materialism. The main theist view asserts a divine creation of each life and a final judgment after death followed by eternity in heaven or hell. Scientific materialism rejects this view and holds that the mind is produced by neurological processes and therefore ceases when the brain dies. A Buddhist approach to such questions offers another alternative, which will be described below. The Buddhist view aims to overcome three mistaken notions that block spiritual development: doubts about whether the mind is a continuum, about whether actions have consequences, and about whether enlightenment is possible.

For one considering a spiritual path, the first crucial question lies in whether the mind ceases with the body's demise or continues on after death. Other questions that follow are if our minds die with our bodies, then why put much effort into spiritual transformation? If our mind is a continuum that survives death, where does it go and what determines the course it takes? Where did the mind come from? When did it begin? What causes it? And what is the nature of the mind?

From a logical standpoint, we cannot say something does not exist simply because it is not an object of mundane sensory awareness. Absence of a perception of a phenomena does not prove the absence of that phenomenon.

Therefore, it would be absurd to assert that the mind ceases when the body dies just because we cannot see its functioning. Neuroscientists are doing increasingly sophisticated work in mapping the brain's functioning, but they are still unable to directly see the mind. Some materialists, therefore, jump to the unsubstantiated conclusion that the mind is only the process of neurology, but this is an assumption, not a fact. Given its invisibility to the scrutiny of our senses, questions remain as to its causes and nature, but awareness itself proves the existence of mind.

Neuroscientists have shown how changes in neurology affect the mind, but they have also shown how mental changes affect neurological functioning. For example, stress and depression can damage the hippocampus, a portion of the brain associated with memory, causing it to shrink and lose cells.[25] In other studies, meditation has been shown to activate and strengthen the prefrontal cortex, which is associated with improved self-regulation skills.[26] Indeed, the empirical evidence of changes in the mind causing changes in the body has burgeoned over the past few decades, but the concept of mind affecting the body is not new. Dharmakirti (600-660 C.E.), a Buddhist logician, argued that while the mind can be influenced by the body, the body can also be influenced by the mind:

The same is true of mind and body.
They coexist with each one's cause assisting
In the arising of the other's result,
Like fire and the liquidity of copper.[27]

When copper melts upon exposure to fire, the fire creates changes in the copper but is of a different substance from the copper. Fire melts the copper, but is not the material cause for the molten copper. The molten copper's material cause is the copper before it melted. Similarly, fire's material cause is a preceding moment of fire. Therefore, fire and copper may influence each other, but they have different material causes.

Likewise, Dharmakirti asserts that, although the mind and body influence each other, they have distinctly different material causes. An example from nature might help to illustrate the meaning of "material cause." Take the relationship between an apple tree and its seed. The material cause for an apple tree is only an apple seed. No other cause can produce it and its seed governs every quality that issues forth into the resultant apple tree. This is what defines the apple seed as the "material cause" of the apple tree. However, the apple seed by itself is insufficient on its own to produce the apple tree. It needs the cooperative conditions of soil, warmth and moisture, which each have their own individual material causes that, when combined with the appropriate seed, form into the apple tree.

Similarly, Dharmakirti argued that the mind needs a similar material cause of mental nature in order to be produced. No other cause but one of a mental nature can produce a moment of mind. In other words mind must be caused by a previous moment of mind. It can be influenced by the body but is not produced by the body. The body has its own unique material causes: the sperm and egg of the parents. These causes for the body are the cooperative conditions that, when combined with the seed of a mental continuum from a previous life, give rise to an embodied being. The logic that follows from this view is that each moment of mind depends on there having been a previous moment of mind to produce it. Therefore, no first moment of mind can be postulated. In other words, the mind is without beginning because any asserted beginning of mind would need to be preceded and produced by a cause of mental nature.[28]

Such logic supports the notion of the mind as a continuum and the Buddhist view of rebirth. Within such a view of the mind, the research of Dr. Ian Stevenson (1918-2007) and others on children with past life memories can be accepted. During his life, Dr. Stevenson of the University of Virginia's Department of Behavioral Medicine and Psychiatry, researched over 3000 cases of children with memories of a past life. For example, in one investigation with records made by researchers before having been verified with historical accounts, a young daughter of school teachers, Subashini Gunasekera—born in Sri Lanka on January 13, 1980—started talking about memories of a previous life in which she had been "trapped" when a hill fell on her house during a rainstorm. She said the town she had lived in when this occurred was Sinhapitiya, Gampola, and that she had a family member named Vasini. She also recounted details about her previous family, such as their having lived on a tea farm next to a hill, and a description of the incident that caused her death.

To her parents' surprise, following the disclosures from Subashini, a relative informed them that there had indeed been a landslide in Sinhapitiya. Later, they were able to obtain a newspaper (published on October 25, 1977) documenting the tragedy, which had occurred on a tea farm during a rainstorm. When Subashini's father took her to visit the site of the tragedy, she became so frightened of becoming trapped again that she stopped the visit before inquiries could be made. Investigators later interviewed Subashini and her family in detail before researching the site at Sinhapitiya. At the site, survivors of the tragedy were interviewed at length and of the 32 details given by Subashini about her previous life, investigators were able to verify all but seven as accurate for the life of a young girl, Devi Mallika, who was killed in the landslide. This includes finding that the name "Vasini" mentioned by

Subashini corresponded to a nickname of Devi Mallika's younger sister.[29] This and many similar cases give empirical evidence of past lives.

Near death experiences in which survivors have memories during periods when they were pronounced dead can also be understood within Dharmakirti's view of the mind. Other psychic phenomena like children who speak unlearned languages and people who display clairvoyance[30] that contradict a materialistic view of the mind can be explained as well. In the former instance, a child with unlearned language could be displaying an ability learned in a previous life; and in the latter instance, an individual with clairvoyance may be displaying an ability of the mind to function beyond the confines of neurology. While the mind is certainly an elusive object of study, its functioning can be examined by each of us within our own daily experiences. Examining our own minds provides an additional doorway for personal exploration to test the accuracy and efficacy of the Buddha's teachings for ourselves.

The Four Noble Truths

In teaching the Four Noble Truths, the Buddha began by teaching the truth of suffering. In his discourses, he described the myriad forms of suffering that unenlightened beings endure in their unending pursuit of happiness. All of these varieties of suffering can be condensed into three general categories called the suffering of suffering, the suffering of change, and the suffering of conditioned existence. The first type of suffering is obvious even to animals and includes encounters with all forms of physical and mental unpleasantness. The second type is more subtle and constitutes the changing nature of our feelings towards the pleasant things we cling to in our quest for fulfillment—they change from sources of temporary respite from one form of suffering into causes of yet another form of suffering. For example, a good meal can change into a cause of indigestion or a close relative can turn into a source of torment and so forth. Subtler still is the suffering of conditioned existence. It is the very nature of our contaminated psycho-physical constituents (so called because they have been born from karma and mental afflictions), which are a vessel for present suffering and which serve as a cause for future suffering due to our creating continued karma and afflictions on their account.

The second truth taught by the Buddha describes the causes of our suffering. In the *Dhammapada*, Buddha says, "Mind is the fore-runner of all things. Mind is chief; and they are of the nature of mind. If, with an evil mind, one speaks or acts, then pain follows one just as the cart follows the horse. Mind is the forerunner of all things. Mind is chief; and they are of the nature of mind. If, with a pure mind, one speaks or acts, then happiness follows one just like the shadow that never leaves."[31] Impure motives and the acts they foster inevitably lead to suffering, while pure states of mind lead to actions which give rise to happiness. It is our afflicted mental states combined with karma (actions) that propel us into various states of suffering as we cycle through birth and death.

Of all the things taught by the Buddha, karma is said to be the most hidden and difficult to examine phenomenon. Other subjects he taught can be confirmed by observation and/or logic. But, because the workings of karma are said to be only knowable to someone who has attained enlightenment, traditionally, the authority of the Buddha's speech is relied upon when approaching this particular topic. However, an interesting case among Dr. Stevenson's studies seems to verify some of the traditional teachings on karma, and might be worth mentioning at this point.

According to the case study, a boy named Wijeratne was born in Ceylon on January 17, 1947 with a deformity to his right breast and arm. His father noticed certain of the boy's features, which were similar to the father's deceased brother, Ratran Hami. When Wijeratne was between two and two and a half years old, he began pacing and talking to himself, saying that his arm was deformed because he murdered his previous life's wife. His mother overheard this along with several other details of the crime, things she had never heard before. When she told her husband about them, he confirmed that they were accurate in describing what had happened to his younger brother, Ratran Hami, who had been executed in 1928 for the murder of his wife, a fact that the father had previously withheld from Wijeratne's mother. The father tried to dissuade Wijeratne from discussing his memories, but Wijeratne continued to talk about them with vividness and detail when asked about his arm. Eventually investigators became involved and took detailed records of his statements, checking them against available history. Since there were court records of Ratran Hami's trial and execution, it was relatively easy to get accurate information. The boy's statements were validated by the historical record.[32]

The Buddha taught that karma, once planted in the mind, leads to various types of effects. One type of effect is a fruition of the action, which in the case of murder, would be a life in a lower form of birth. In Wijeratne's case, this can be seen in his memory of the 18 and a half year gap between the execution of Ratran Hami and the birth of Wijeratne, in which Wijeratne recalled having dropped into a pit of fire after the execution (perhaps a brief period in a hell realm) and then having "flitted through the air and perched on tree tops" (presumably a life as a bird). A second kind of karmic effect is one that is similar to the cause, which in the case of murder would be a shortened life and/ or health problems. Wijeratne not only had the physical deformity, which he attributed to having stabbed his wife, but he also began to have psychotic breaks as he entered his teenage years when rejected by girls (during which time he would have the delusion of being a bird). A third type of karmic effect is an effect functionally similar to the cause, which in the case of murder would be a future inclination towards the same behavior. Wijeratne displayed this aspect in his insistence that his wife in his former life had deserved to be killed for having stood him up on their wedding day and that he would do it again (an attitude that he eventually changed as he struggled with the karmic effects of his former crime).

Another aspect of karma that seems illustrated by Wijeratne's case is known as "throwing karma," consisting of the last, predominating impulse in life, which determines the type and course of one's future life. In this case, after the judge had sentenced Ratran Hami to death, Ratran reportedly told his brother "I am not afraid. I know that I will have to die. I am only worried about you," adding later that he "would return." This might partly account for the bizarre coincidence of Ratran Hami eventually returning as his brother's son. In any case, nature rarely affords a glimpse into its hidden processes, but from a Buddhist viewpoint, this case seems to offer such a window.

It is important to gain certainty about the workings of rebirth and karma in order to fully comprehend our current predicament and gain a resolve to find freedom from it. Like a doctor diagnosing an illness, the Buddha began his teachings on the four truths by describing the truth of the problems we endure and follows with an assessment of their true causes—impure actions performed with afflicted states of mind resulting in uncontrolled rebirth into states of unhappiness and suffering. It is this second truth of the causes of suffering that provides insight into the possibility of a solution. If a doctor can identify the cause of an illness, by removing that cause he can effect a cure. Similarly, by clearly seeing the factors that bind us to suffering, we can begin the process of eliminating them.

Understanding this gives rise to being able to comprehend the third truth of cessation. When the Buddha became enlightened he said, "The chain is broken, the emotions stilled. The stream of impurities is dry and runs no more. As the chain is destroyed, suffering is ended."[33] He also said, "Deep, peaceful, away from all extremes, clearly luminous and uncompounded; I have found the nectar-like Dharma which cannot be understood by anyone to whom it is shown, so I should remain alone and silent in the forest."[34] It was only when requested that he began to teach the path to the Dharma he had realized. The Buddha eliminated his own causes of suffering and then, moved by compassion, undertook the task of teaching others how to do the same. He saw that everyone has the innate potential to awaken and become perfectly enlightened. It is a potential that lies within the very nature of our minds. In itself, mind is not inherently good or bad, but rather, it is colored by the factors with which it associates. Anger and vengefulness can make it cruel. Love and compassion can make it gentle and courageous. Desire enslaves it and ignorance bewilders it. Insight combined with meditative equipoise sets it free.

In the Perfection of Wisdom Sutras, the Buddha said, "Mind is devoid of mind, because the nature of mind is clear-light."[35] In other words, mind is devoid of any autonomous, independent self-nature. It arises interdependently moment-by-moment and therefore exists without being self-existent. Due to the mind's lack of an independent, autonomous nature, it is possible that one's mind can awaken, become free of its defilements, and enter into ultimate peace. Just like water can be distilled from its pollutants, the mind can be purified of mental afflictions and ignorance to reveal its pristine, clear light nature. Like a lake, there are many levels of the mind to clean, including its murky depths. Like a sky, uncontaminated by the clouds that course through it, the mind does not necessarily need to be colored by the afflictions to which it has become accustomed. Therefore, like a garden, our minds can be tended, weeded, nurtured and cultivated until they become filled with only positive states, and cleansed of all defilements, culminating in full awakening.

With the above understanding, one can eventually eliminate doubts about whether the mind is a continuum, about whether actions have consequences, and about whether enlightenment is possible. To do so takes extended effort, listening to repeated discourses on the Buddha's teachings (the Dharma), thinking deeply about the meanings with detailed analysis, and meditating on what is learned. With the resulting realizations that the mind is a continuum, that actions have consequences, and that enlightenment is possible, the teachings on the stages of the path to enlightenment become easily understood and logical.

The Buddha's final words before passing beyond were, "Brethren, all things decay. Be mindful, be righteous and be vigilant. Be lamps unto yourselves. Transient are all compounded things. Therefore, strive earnestly to attain perfection."[36]

The Stages of the Path to Enlightenment

The basic principles of Buddhism, described above, provide a foundation for understanding the stages of the path, which is the second of the two main subject matters presented in the Water and Wood Shastras. Gungthang Rinpoche's verses on the stages of the path to enlightenment *(Lamrim)* can be found in verses 80 through 138 of the Water Shastra and in verses 1 through 35 of the Wood Shastra. *Lamrim* is a systematic organization of all Buddha's myriad teachings in which "the rivers of instruction from thousands of scriptural volumes are gathered together."[37] Two major lineages of instruction are combined: the teachings on the vast activities of Bodhisattvas[38] and the instructions on the profound view of voidness.[39] The former instructions were passed from the Buddha to Maitreya to Asanga and then to a series of lineage teachers up to the present day. The latter were passed from the Buddha to Manjushri to Nagarjuna and through successive disciples up to now.[40] These streams of instruction were combined into the *Lamrim* system by Dipamkara Atisha (982-1054) in his groundbreaking text, "The Lamp of the Path to Enlightenment" (Sanskrit: *Bodhipathapradipa*; Tibetan: *byang chub lam gyi sgron ma*). Many *Lamrim* texts were composed after that, following the prototype of the steps set down by Master Atisha, because of the benefits afforded by such a presentation. Je Tsongkapa mentions four particular benefits of the *Lamrim* approach:

> *We can realize that all the teachings are non-contradictory,*
> *All the scriptures without exception will appear as personal advice,*

We will easily find Buddha's intent,
And we will be protected from the abyss of the great mistake.[41]

When Buddha taught in India, he spoke at the level of the disciples he was leading at the moment. Therefore, when reading the vast collection of his discourses, the following misunderstanding might arise, "The Buddha says to practice one way in this discourse, but seems to be saying something contradictory in another." Such thoughts are dispelled in those with a thorough overview of the entire path to enlightenment. Once one grasps the steps on the path, it is easy to see how different levels of spiritual development call for unique approaches, and therefore, how the Buddha's teachings are actually non-contradictory. Furthermore, with the understanding afforded by studying *Lamrim*, every discourse you read will be seen as essential to your practice, so that you can begin to utilize the treasury of instructions contained in the scriptures. This will open the door to realizing Buddha's purpose in each thing he taught, and prevent the great mistake of abandoning any portion of his teachings, all of which are essential for attaining the ultimate goal of the path.

At the beginning of the teachings on *Lamrim* there are instructions on how to teach and on how to listen. An old Tibetan proverb says, "The water of knowledge will not stay on the mountain peak of pride." In contrast, as

Gungthang Rinpoche says:

> *An observant, intelligent person*
> *Will absorb the good qualities of others.*
> *The gently flowing brook gathers flowers*
> *As it murmurs through the pure meadowlands.*[42]

Acquiring knowledge from one's teacher is like absorbing their good qualities. Therefore, to prepare the mind for contemplating the stages of the path, both teacher and disciple should begin by setting their motivations. The usual analogies to help with this are the "faults of the three pots" and "six considerations." In the former, the student is encouraged to avoid being like an upside-down pot, in which close-mindedness or distraction prevents the nectar of the teachings from pouring in. One also should eliminate the faults of an upright pot that is filled with the impurities of negative motives for listening, which will spoil the virtues that would otherwise accrue. The path of Dharma is not about making money. It is not about becoming famous or making people like you. It is not about dominating others or feeling superior to them. It is a path to finding inner peace, developing compassionate wisdom, and attaining an ultimate state of well-being for oneself and others. Only this latter goal is an appropriate motivation for contemplating *Lamrim*. The last faulty pot analogy depicts an upright, clean pot with a hole in the bottom that allows the contents to escape. This illustrates the futility of listening with a distracted mind that immediately forgets the points learned.

Instead of the above three faults, one is encouraged to practice the six considerations of imagining oneself as a patient afflicted by suffering and its causes, the Buddha as the consummate doctor able to cure one's ailment, the Dharma as medicine able to affect the cure, and the Sangha[43] as nurses to help one apply the medicine properly. The final two points are to use the medicine as instructed, and then once having appreciated its efficacy, to help preserve it and disseminate it to others. In short, a student intent on realizing the path to enlightenment should endeavor to be honest, unbiased, discerning, wishing for a true path, respectful, and open to looking unflinchingly at his or her mind. Most importantly, it is crucial to develop conviction that the state of Buddhahood[44] is attainable by anyone willing to develop the body and mind to their fullest potentials. There are two aspects to the aspiration for such enlightenment: the compassionate wish to liberate all beings from suffering and the realization that one must become a Buddha in order to accomplish such a noble goal. When one seeks enlightenment with this dual goal in mind, one becomes a Bodhisattva, and again, this is the best motivation for approaching these teachings.

The actual teachings on the stages of the path are divided into three basic categories pertaining to three levels of spiritual development. They form an outline on how to systematically develop the various levels of spiritual realization Bodhisattvas must accomplish on their journey to Buddhahood. Consider an infant being raised by a loving parent. First the child must learn to trust the parent in order to be properly mentored. Then the child has to learn the basics of self-care. As the child matures, more effort goes into training for long-term goals, and finally, as maturity is attained, he or she learns to care for others as well as for him or herself. Similarly, the levels of trainings for aspirants are divided into small, medium, and great scopes, but all are equally necessary for successful completion of the path.

Preliminary Topics to the Path to Enlightenment

The root of correct positive causation producing
Every goodness in this and future lives
Is to strive to properly serve the holy spiritual guide,
Who shows you the path, in thought and action.
Seeing this, don't give up pleasing him
With the offering of practicing just as instructed,
Even for the sake of your life;

I the yogi have practiced this way,
You who seek liberation should do likewise.[45]
—Je Tsongkapa

In the above analogy of a child's development, the most important factor ensuring the child's safety and well-being is the continual care of a loving parent through each stage of development. This corresponds to the *Lamrim* teachings on how to find and properly follow a spiritual master. Also important is a child's sense of worth and potential, which can be compared to teachings on recognizing and taking advantage of this perfect human life. These two topics were not formally included by Dipamkara Atisha in his *Lamp of the Path to Enlightenment*, but were extensively explained by Je Tsongkapa and other *Lamrim* authors as the very fundamentals of the steps of the path.

Finding a qualified spiritual guide is the basis of the path and the lifeblood of higher stages of practice. A qualified guide can help protect us from a lower rebirth,[46] give instructions on how to free ourselves from cyclic existence,[47] show us the road to higher rebirth, help us learn to heal our mental afflictions, and bestow techniques for developing our spiritual potential to its fullest. However, it is very important from the beginning to be discerning about how we choose a spiritual guide and about how we relate to them. Rightfully, many are suspicious of people who present themselves as spiritual guides. History is full of sad examples of charlatans, crooks, narcissists, tyrants and psychotics parading in the garb of religion. Therefore, for a sane person, there is just cause to be cautious. Gungthang Rinpoche concurs when he says:

A loud, untamed preacher
Whose mind is worse than a butcher
Is like the winter mist;
When it gathers in the valleys, it is especially cold.[48]

Therefore, it is good to approach one's search with some guidelines. Maitreya, in his *Ornament for the Mahayana Sutras (mdo sde'i rgyan),* mentions ten qualities that a high level spiritual guide should have: tamed by morality, at peace through concentration, thoroughly pacified by wisdom, fluent in scriptural learning, holding a correct view of emptiness, possessing greater positive qualities than the student, skilled in guiding disciples, moved to teach by compassion instead of wanting profit or respect, filled with joyful effort to mentor, and tolerant of shortcomings in students. If one finds such a guide, it is incumbent on one to develop a positive relationship through giving support to the teacher's endeavors, and most importantly, by practicing what they teach. It is said that the virtues of properly attending a spiritual guide are vast and the negativity of disrespecting such a relationship quite severe. Gungthang Rinpoche comments on this as follows:

If you rely upon a wish-granting tree,
All that you need and want comes down like rain.
Similarly, if you rely on a holy spiritual friend,
A mass of goodness is spontaneously achieved.

Those who disrespect their spiritual guide,
Though understanding a hundred scriptures, derive no benefit.
Throw dry wood into water for a hundred years, yet
It is impossible for it to sprout leaves and branches.[49]

The second topic that lays a foundation for the practices that follow concerns realizing the rarity and value of your present situation as a human. If you have a diamond in your hand, it is important to know what you have, otherwise you might lose or waste it. Just as a child must become aware of his or her worth and potential in order to take care of his or her health and develop skills for a fulfilling life, the spiritual aspirant must learn to recognize this rare and precious opportunity of being human as the gateway to higher births, ultimate well-being, and total enlightenment. This builds the confidence and self-care necessary for mastering the stages that follow.

According to Buddha's teachings, right now the majority of beings are suffering in unfortunate realms of existence: in hells, as tormented spirits, or as animals. But you are not. Some have lives of such privilege and luxury that they are unmotivated to pursue any spiritual development, but this is not your condition. You haven't been born in a time or place where these teachings are not available. You haven't been born without full faculties, nor with views that block you from considering the Buddha's teachings. These conditions are called the "eight leisures."

Instead, you have been born human, in a place and time that allow access to the teachings, with complete mental and physical faculties allowing study and practice, and without severe misdeeds that could block your progress. Most importantly, if you have some confidence in the validity of the Buddha's teachings, then you can make use of the precious opportunity afforded by this life. The Buddha appeared in this world, he taught the Dharma, and his teachings remain and are still being taught. Moreover, there are still people who support the teachings and practitioners. These factors are called the "ten fortunes."

So, from a Buddhist point of view, as a human living during the present time, you are really quite rich in spiritual potential and have everything you need to develop that potential to its fullest. If you use this opportunity well, it is taught that you can prevent a miserable rebirth after you die; or better, you can free yourself from suffering completely and forever; or best, you can become fully enlightened in order to attain ultimate well-being not only for yourself, but for all sentient beings. The Buddha gave analogies such as that of a blind turtle in the ocean having the fortune to stick its neck through the opening of a yoke floating on the surface, a bean sticking on a crystal wall, seeing a star at noon, a mustard seed staying on the tip of a needle and so forth in order to illustrate the rarity of finding all the conditions that produce the leisure and fortune of this human life.[50] Gungthang Rinpoche adds:

> *If the essence of this leisure and fortune is not taken,*
> *It is no different from having taken an animal's birth.*
> *If the mango fruit is not enjoyed,*
> *What is its distinction from a castor oil plant?[51]*

The Small Scope Stage

> *By whatever means, whoever strives*
> *For merely the happiness of cyclic existence,*
> *Seeking their own benefit,*
> *Know these beings as the least.[52]*
> *—Jowo Atisha*

Most small infants strive for immediate gratification and get quite upset when desires are not quickly attained. Similarly, a person of small capacity is concerned predominantly with desires for his or her own happiness in this life. Death is rarely considered by such individuals, and when it is considered, often it serves as an incentive to indulge in pleasure seeking with logic like "live for the moment," and "you only go around once in life." But, of course, if the Buddhist view of rebirth is correct, these rationalizations are tragically mistaken. Such logic undermines taking the benefit of finding a perfect human life and often increases torment as people chase after elusive and fleeting sensual pleasures, only to find that their desires turn into intense cravings, sometimes culminating in addictions. In some cases, people turn to crime, to drugs and alcohol, to greed, to hedonism, to fame mongering and so forth in a desperate search for some satisfaction.

In the *Apannaka Sutta* (*The Incontrovertible Teaching*), the Buddha describes nihilistic and eternalistic[53] views of existence that can lead to a depraved life and unfortunate rebirth due to believing that there is "…no fruit or result of good and bad actions…no evil and outcome of evil… no cause or condition for the defilement of beings."[54] He also points out that if one has correct views of karma, and lives a wholesome life, happiness is experienced in the here and now due to being stable, trusted and respected. In addition, one's wholesome actions form the basis for confidence in a good future life. On the other hand, if a person lives destructively without respect or care, life becomes full of contention, discontent and tragedy. Then when death comes, there will be the additional tragedy of an unfortunate rebirth.

So, a spiritual aspirant of initial or small scope must train to overcome grasping at the concerns of this life and learn to strive for the happiness of future lives. Most of us are consumed by preoccupations about our present conditions. We crave wealth, pleasure, praise and fame, pursuing them even if it risks one's life. In contrast, we are deeply troubled when faced by loss, discomfort, criticism, and ill repute. These are called the "eight worldly dharmas"[55] that drive most human behavior. From a karmic point of view, pursuing these desires and emotions plants seeds for future misery, and from a psychological point of view, our dissatisfaction with the here and now increases as we make these the focus of our life's goals. Frustrations mount as our increasing drive for immediate gratification is repeatedly thwarted by the inevitable obstacles that arise in daily life.

In contrast to such a meaningless approach to life, there are the "ten innermost jewels" of the Kadampa Geshes,[56] who aimed their lives solely at spiritual practice, aimed their practice at life as a beggar (in order to overcome worries about poverty), aimed life as a beggar at death (in order to overcome worries about starvation and so on), and aimed death at being alone in an empty cave (in order to overcome preoccupations about dying alone without someone to provide care). These four "aims" constitute the first four of the "ten innermost jewels."

The next three jewels use the analogy of a *vajra*, which is a Sanskrit term (Tibetan: *rdo rje*) that can be translated as adamantine or diamond. [57] "Send the ungraspable vajra ahead," meaning they would not allow themselves to be coerced away from their path even by crying loved ones. "Lay the unabashed vajra behind," meaning they would not let criticism about their choice sway them. "Keep the wisdom vajra at your side," meaning they used every moment for practice.

The final three of the ten jewels focus on outcomes. As a result of such a thorough pursuit of the path, the Kadampa Geshes braced themselves to be "cast out from the ranks of men" and to "enter the life of dogs," meaning that they would accept the social rebuke that might come as a result of their spiritual focus and that they also would accept the humblest of necessities for living in order to allow more time for practice. The final jewel is the fulfillment of their path, "to enter the ranks of the divine," which in its highest form means attaining enlightenment within a single lifetime.

In order to begin the process of unlocking the mind from its preoccupation with immediate gratification and worldly pursuits, the Buddha taught extensively on impermanence. It is due to not remembering our impermanence that we think only of this life's happiness, postpone spiritual practice, run after temporal pleasures, and enter into negative actions to get what we want. In contrast, if we can become mindful of our own approaching death, it will help us prioritize the meaningful over the meaningless, the virtuous over the non-virtuous, and to immediately set out on our spiritual path. Death will definitely come to us, our lifespan is diminishing with each day that passes, and there is little time left for spiritual practice. There is no fixed time as to when we will die; it could come at any moment. Our bodies are fragile and there are many causes of death, but the things we need to support life are difficult to acquire. When death comes, our friends can't help us, our wealth and position are left behind, and our cherished bodies cease to function. Only our karma accompanies us through death as it shapes us into what we will become next. Gungthang Rinpoche says:

From the very moment of birth, not abiding,
You head toward the mouth of the Lord of Death,
Just like a stream, which in each moment,
Flows irreversibly into the sea.[58]

One great teacher[59] said that we do not need to get a travel visa or an airplane ticket to visit the lower realms of existence; all we need is for this breath leaving our nostrils to cease from returning. At the time of our death, if our karma leads us to a hellish destiny, how will we endure the pain? Scriptures describe the lives of beings in hell realms as being extremely long in duration and as filled with horrors of every type. While we might find this hard to believe, we can see the temporary hells that our fellow humans go through in the hands of murderers, during warfare, and when calamities occur. From a Buddhist perspective, all such tragedies are arranged by karma and we have a huge storehouse of such karma from our deeds in this and previous lives.

Another destiny to avoid is a life as an animal. Since the mind is in a fluid/subtle state as we go through the death process, it can take on whatever form karma molds for it, including the forms of the multitude of creatures we can see on this planet. Relatively few animals live with the comfort of being a pet. Most live in the eat-or-be-eaten world of the wild. If domesticated, many are beaten, worked or trapped, and many are killed for their flesh and fur. Those who escape torment by humans are subject to the bitter cold of winter and often tormented by thirst, hunger, and the elements. From a Buddhist perspective, the worst feature of being born as an animal is the inability to access the teachings because of limited capacity for language and diminished intelligence.

Yet a third unfortunate destination is called the hungry ghost realm, which is described in the scriptures as a realm of impoverished spirits, constantly tormented by intense hunger, thirst, and craving in a barren place where food and drink are unavailable. These three lower realms are said to be densely populated and are described as having been our most frequent dwelling places through the infinite string of our past lifetimes. Furthermore, since beings in the lower realms tend to engage in negative actions like killing in order to survive, once fallen, it is very difficult and rare to re-emerge into a higher destiny. So, now that we have found this precious human life, what can we do to prevent a return to a lower form of life? Gungthang Rinpoche comments:

> *The sheltering refuge from those great fears*
> *Is none other than the infallible supreme Three Gems.*
> *Carried by a river's current,*
> *Only a boatman is sure to save you.*[60]

The "Three Gems" are the Buddha, Dharma and Sangha. As mentioned previously, the Buddha was able to eradicate suffering and its causes from the root and thus attain a state of fearlessness and ultimate well-being. If he had not attained this, he would not be able to help us, just as a drowning person would be unable to rescue someone else who is sinking. He also was skilled in leading others to the state beyond suffering. In addition he cultivated a compassion that is impartial and therefore helps all seeking protection. Since he awakened his mind completely, his omniscient knowledge allowed him to see our situation clearly, and since he consummated all enlightened activities, his reach and abilities to help were unimpeded. These and many other qualities make him the supreme refuge for all who are still trapped in the cycle of existence.

The ultimate refuge from suffering is the Dharma. At a relative level, this refers to the teachings spoken by the Buddha in order to lead others beyond suffering. In an ultimate sense, Dharma refers to the realizations that come from studying and practicing the Buddha's teachings, in particular, those on cessations of afflicted states of mind and cognitive distortions. If we can gain these internal types of Dharma, they become our ultimate protection.

The Sangha refers to the community of practitioners who help guide us along the path. At a relative level it can refer to a group of monks or nuns, and at an ultimate level, it refers to any Bodhisattva who has reached the path of seeing or beyond.[61]

When Gungthang Rinpoche compares these three sources of refuge to a boatman, he makes a crucial point that can prevent us from overestimating or underestimating the abilities of refuge. Unlike an omnipotent savior who determines whether one will sink or swim in existence, here the savior is seen as a guide who shows the way to safety. It is karma that determines whether we sink or swim. A boatman can rescue us and guide us to safer shores, but if we decline his services, we sink or swim by our own actions. Therefore, proper trust is essential to our path. Well-founded trust points us in a safe direction and allows enlightened beings to guide us. If a disobedient child rejects parental guidance, there is little the parent can do to help the child.

The way we can ensure our connection with the three sources of refuge is to rely on good teachers, listen to their Dharma instructions, practice in accord with what we learn, withdraw from chasing sensory pleasures, develop compassion towards beings, and keep within the precepts of refuge. The precepts of refuge include avoiding mistaken ideas and teachers who might coerce us to stray from the path, and to keep from harming others. In contrast, by maintaining reverence for enlightened beings, their scriptures, and the community of practitioners, one will continue to connect to sources of refuge and receive guidance along the path. It is good to recall the qualities of the three sources of refuge repeatedly, taking refuge several times each day and night, and especially before engaging in activities. Traditionally,

Buddhists will offer the first portion of their food to them before eating and also at times make other more extensive offerings. In short, refuge can and should become the central principal of one's practice.

The benefits of practicing this way are said to be enormous. The scriptures describe such rewards as vastly increasing one's store of virtue, obtaining temporal and ultimate joy, gaining concentration and purity, gaining protection from negative forces, and developing other positive spiritual qualities. In addition, the act of taking refuge is often considered the time when one becomes a Buddhist, and thus one becomes a suitable vessel for taking vows, reduces negative karma, avoids a lower rebirth, accomplishes goals, and can quickly attain Buddhahood. However, Gungthang Rinpoche warns:

> *If you seek out the Supreme Three, practice with zeal*
> *Their precepts on karma and its effects, what to accept and reject.*
> *Though you rely on a captain,*
> *If you do not stay in the boat, how will you be delivered?*[62]

This introduces the next subject of the small scope stage contemplations: karma. Karma, as mentioned previously, is a complex subject. According to Buddhist scriptures, it has four general characteristics of being certain, magnifying, not giving effects if it is not committed, and not perishing.

Its certainty means that unwholesome actions definitely produce only suffering and wholesome actions produce only happiness. It magnifies in that the propensities of even small actions increase over time and can eventually produce expansive effects. If you have not performed a particular karmic action, you will not experience its result. And fourthly, karmic seeds endure if left unaddressed, until they give their effects. As Gungthang Rinpoche says:

Karma collected from beginningless time,
Though a hundred eons pass, is never wasted.
The fruit of the Tala tree might be withered for a thousand years,
Yet if touched by moisture, it will germinate.[63]

There are ten paths of action that Buddha particularly warned against. Three of them constitute physical actions: killing, stealing, and sexual misconduct. Four are verbal deeds: lying, saying divisive things, abusive speech, and speaking meaninglessly. The last three are mental acts: covetousness, holding malice, and maintaining wrong views. As mentioned previously, the results of such misdeeds can be fruitions resulting in a lower rebirth. They can also be concordant. For example, the concordant results of killing is a shortened lifespan and for stealing it is poverty. Abusive speech results in being verbally abused. Not being listened to results from speaking meaninglessly. Desire leads to discontent, malice to contentiousness, and wrong views to confusion.[64] Results can also be environmental, for example, being reborn into inhospitable, barren lands, and so forth, if one has harmed others.

These ten misdeeds can have more or less impact depending on such things as the intensity of the mental afflictions that lead to them, the severity of the deed performed, the frequency with which a deed is enacted, the degree of the wrong view that compels it, and the object towards whom it is directed. The most severe misdeeds are said to ripen as a rebirth in hell, medium-level misdeeds result in a rebirth as a hungry spirit, and smaller misdeeds result in an animal rebirth. One can reduce the negative effects of such misdeeds by purifying them with regret, confession, purification practices, and future restraint. However, it is best if one guards against any such wrongdoing in the first place by recollection, awareness and caution.

Projecting karma, which correlates to the most powerful impulse engaging the mind at the time of death, determines the type of future life one will assume, while completing karma determines the quality of one's conditions in the next life. It is said that one who dies with a virtuous state of mind does not feel much discomfort in the dying process and experiences pleasant visions in the transition between death and the next life (Tibetan: *bar do*). In contrast, one who dies with a non-virtuous state of mind feels great pain and terror at the time of death and experiences nightmare-like visions during the transition between death and rebirth while falling towards an unfortunate destiny. Therefore, it is crucial to practice vigilantly in order to develop wholesome states of mind and positive actions while we are alive, and to cultivate refuge and a virtuous state of mind at the time of death.

One of initial capacity is seen to have mastered the prescribed meditation practices when preoccupations of happiness for this life are replaced by a constant focus on pursuing one's well-being for future lifetimes. It is a path shared in common with more advanced spiritual aspirants because a higher birth is essential for making progress on the path, and is therefore necessary for all levels of practice. In particular, it is essential to create as much virtuous karma as possible through the physical actions of preserving life, enhancing the wealth of others, and maintaining appropriate sexual boundaries. One also accumulates positive karma through actions of positive speech, such as speaking honestly with words that build harmony, as well as communicating respectfully and meaningfully. There is also good karma generated through the mental actions of cultivating contentment rather than craving, compassion instead of hostility, and developing wisdom which uproots wrong views. Such virtuous actions are enhanced by taking and guarding the vows of individual liberation, which help ensure a safe course towards a higher rebirth and liberation.[65]

The Medium Scope Stage

Turning away from samsara's happiness
And refraining from negative actions,
Those who strive for only their own peace,
Such beings are known as middling.[66]
–Jowo Atisha

As healthy children mature and master self-care, their sights naturally fix on long-term goals. Similarly, as spiritual aspirants become accustomed to thinking beyond death and begin to train in the practices of purification and virtue, it is natural for them to seek a more stable form of happiness than merely a higher rebirth. From a Buddhist point of view, we have experienced higher births many times in our past lives, but all the pleasures they have afforded us in the past are now lost. Moreover, if we waste our virtuous karma on the mundane worldly pleasures found in higher births, eventually this karma will be depleted and we will fall again to a lower birth. Therefore, it is only logical to strive for a permanent solution to suffering and its causes. Je Tsongkapa states:

If you don't try to contemplate the disadvantages of the truth of suffering,
A true aspiration for liberation will not arise.
If you don't contemplate how the origin of suffering places and keeps you in this cycle of existence, you will not understand the way to cut the cycle's root.
Therefore, seek disillusionment, renunciation of samsara,
And cherish the knowledge of what binds you to its cycle.
I the yogi have practiced this way,
You who seek liberation should do likewise.[67]

Without true renunciation, we are like prisoners, content with our cells, unmotivated to look for a way to freedom. Therefore, the Buddha taught various contemplations on the sufferings of cyclic existence in order to help us become disenchanted with it. For instance, all of us experience the eight sufferings of birth, old age, illness, death, encountering the unpleasant, being separated from the pleasant, not getting what we want, and the suffering of "the appropriated aggregates." This last form of suffering refers to the impure constituents of our body and mind that we have acquired based on our past karma contaminated by cognitive distortions and afflicted states of mind. Such a contaminated body and mind are vessels for present suffering due to the various harms one encounters in life, and for future suffering due to the karma we create with them. It is the wish to remove the suffering associated with having such contaminated aggregates that constitutes the real definition of renunciation.

There are also another six forms of suffering mentioned by the Buddha: the uncertainties of cyclic existence, our insatiable desires for its pleasures, the repeated casting off of bodies, the incessant taking of rebirth, descending again and again from high status to low, and ultimately being alone as we journey through life and death. All of these various forms of suffering can be subsumed into the three forms of suffering mentioned previously: the suffering of suffering, the suffering of change, and the suffering of conditioned existence.

In addition, the Buddha mentioned specific types of suffering that beings encounter depending on the realm of their rebirth. Among humans, rich people predominantly suffer mentally while the poor encounter more physical hardships. The powerful oppress the weak; many suffer from brutality, thirst, hunger, heat and cold, and most endure worry and fear along with other forms of mental distress. The sufferings of the three lower realms were mentioned briefly above, but the scriptures also mention divine realms within the cycle of existence where beings encounter sufferings from things like warfare, afflicted mental states, approaching death, and the ensuing anxiety about loss of status and falling into lower realms. Therefore, within samsara, there is no safe place. Everywhere is marked with impermanence, dissatisfaction and suffering. True renunciation arises when one develops a constant wish, day and night, to gain freedom from the cycle of birth and death. Gungthang Rinpoche comments:

> *Desire is a salty river,*
> *No matter how much you drink, your thirst is never quenched.*
> *Like a goose iced on a lake,*
> *Rouse the sorrow wanting sure escape from samsara.*[68]

Once one has established a firm resolution to seek freedom from the cycle of existence, the next step is to identify the factors that bind one in samsara in order to extinguish them. This is similar to a prisoner examining the routines of the prison guards as he plans his escape. The Buddha taught that the mental afflictions, particularly craving, are the fetters that bind us to the prison of our contaminated mental and physical aggregates, which are of the nature of suffering. Our mental afflictions are the cooperative conditions—like the soil, warmth and moisture—that provide fertile ground in which the seeds of negative karma can germinate and grow. Dharmakirti in his *Commentary on the "Compendium of Valid Cognition"* says:

> *The karma of one who has transcended craving for existence*
> *Lacks the potency to project another birth*
> *Because its cooperative conditions are gone...,*
> *The aggregates will arise again if you have craving.*[69]

The mental afflictions disturb mental peace. Attachment increases craving and reduces contentment; anger disrupts peace of mind and burns away virtues; jealousy torments; pride inflates self-importance, diminishing others, and leads to alienation; ignorance blinds; and doubt impedes progress by causing vacillation about the path. These and the multitude of other disturbing mental factors all have their roots in the misconception that holds to this perishable assemblage of our mental and physical constituents as if it were an independent self. By holding to these aggregates as if they exist from their own side and constitute a self, we delineate "myself" from others. Thus we become attached to what we see as ours and hostile or indifferent to all else. Threats to what we see as "me and mine" and obstacles to what we want lead to anger and hostility. Jealousy, pride and a wide assortment of other afflictions and wrong views grow out of this. Dharmakirti comments:

> *Once there is a self, there is an idea of an other.*
> *On behalf of self and other, there is attachment and hostility.*
> *All the faults come about*
> *In association with these.*[70]

On the basis of latent predispositions for the various afflictions within our minds, bolstered by contact with sensory objects, negative social influences, wrong views we have learned, and negative habits we have become accustomed to, we naturally give rise to afflicted cognitive distortions about reality: imagining the impure to be pure, suffering to be happiness, the impermanent to be permanent, and that which is without self-nature as having a self. As we follow these afflicted states of mind, we harm ourselves and others by undermining ethical conduct and creating karma leading to a lower rebirth. In short, by clinging to ourselves and to temporal pleasures, we create new causes for the various sufferings of cyclic existence. Therefore, the mental afflictions are our real enemies. They are like guards holding us in the prison of cyclic existence.

Since the underpinning for all of our afflictions is the misapprehension of an independent self, those who can directly ascertain selflessness begin the process of extricating themselves from cyclic existence. By perfecting meditation on selflessness, all the afflictions are gradually eliminated and one produces causes that cut the shackles of *samsara*. Otherwise, without such a realization, all the karma we create, whether virtuous and leading to higher realms, non-virtuous and leading to lower realms, or invariable and leading to form and formless realm states,[71] will keep us within samsara and therefore bound to repeated birth, death, uncertainty, fear, dissatisfaction and suffering.

It is important to know the twelve links of dependent arising in order to deepen one's understanding of how cyclic existence operates, more fully comprehend how causes lead to effects, and further one's aspiration to seek freedom. The first link is ignorance, which is shown in paintings as a blind man using a staff for support as he stumbles into an uncertain future. There are two main categories of ignorance this refers to—primarily, the mistaken view that this perishable assemblage of our mental and physical constituents constitutes an independent self, and secondly, not understanding cause and effect. Based on this blindness, one enters into activities producing unripened karma, the second link, which is depicted artistically as a man molding clay into pots. Just like a potter fashioning clay, with each stained impulse[72] and action, we form different types of positive and negative karma resulting in higher and lower rebirths. The third link, consciousness, is portrayed as a monkey eating fruit and dropping seeds on the ground as he swings from tree to tree. This represents the consciousness permeated by karma developed in one lifetime entering into rebirth in a future life fashioned by the karmic impulses from its previous existence and stained by ignorance. These first three links are the unripened karma planted with each moment of thought, each of which has the power to produce a future life.

The fourth link, called "name and form," is painted as a boat with four passengers, representing the body (the boat) and mind (the passengers of feeling, discrimination, compositional factors, and consciousness) of the new life as it forms due to the stained ripening of karma. One can be reborn from a womb, an egg, from warmth and moisture, or from miraculous circumstances (for example, when born as a hell-being or in the form realm), and therefore, the development of the fifth link, known as the "six sources," can vary according to what kind of birth one takes. This link is portrayed as an empty house with doors and windows. These openings represent the formation of the mental and sense faculties that produce the sensation of their respective objects. The sixth link, contact, is depicted as two lovers in embrace, and represents the coming together of the sense objects, the sense faculties, and the sensory consciousnesses in order to form perceptions of pleasant, unpleasant and neutral sensations. This process results in the seventh link—the feelings of pleasure and pain, as well as neutral feelings—painted as a man with an arrow in his eye. These four links are results, whereas the previous three are causes. Together, these seven links (three causal and four resultant) represent the projection of karma.

The eighth link, initial desire, is symbolized by a man sipping beer. Feelings accompanied by ignorance lead to desire for more encounters with pleasurable sensations as well as the desire to avoid meeting that which is unpleasant. As one becomes habituated to such desires, the ninth link manifests—grasping—represented by a monkey reaching to grasp a piece of fruit. Grasping ripens latent karma, preparing it and bringing it to maturation. It includes grasping for sensory pleasures, holding onto to wrong views, clinging to notions of a self and to negative habits of mistaken morality. The eighth and ninth links bring unripened karma to fully develop its potential, which constitutes the tenth link, existence. This tenth link is depicted as a pregnant woman ready to produce a new life, which represents the fully ripened karma ready to produce rebirth.

The last two links are results. Birth, the eleventh link, is drawn as a woman giving birth and represents the rebirth of contaminated aggregates produced under the influence of karma and mental afflictions. Once born, we inevitably face the twelfth link--old age and death--due again to the power of karma and afflictions. This is depicted as a corpse being carried off to the charnel grounds. These last two resultant links and the three causal links that precede them represent the completion of karma.

The shortest possible scenario for these links to fully unfold is when the first, eighth and ninth links (afflicted mental states) and links two and ten (afflicted karma) are planted within a single lifetime; and then the remaining seven links (afflicted results) ripen during a second life. It is also possible for the process to take three or more lifetimes before the development of the factors that project a birth are actualized. All of these links are held in the jaws of impermanence and take us into various states of misery. But, by defeating the first link of ignorance, we can halt the progression of the other links because each succeeding link is produced by the one preceding it. It is by fully understanding dependent origination that ignorance can be destroyed.

There is a symbolic painting, said to have been conceived by the Buddha, which depicts the entire process of these twelve links, the realms of rebirth to which they lead, the primary afflictions fueling them, and the monster of impermanence devouring everyone held in its grasp. It is called "The Wheel of Life." Above the depiction of the monster of impermanence holding the wheel of existence in his mouth, there is an image of the Buddha pointing to the full moon. This image represents the path to enlightenment (the Buddha pointing the way), and the resultant enlightenment represented by the full moon. The Buddha added two verses to go along with the painting that say:

Commence the higher and cast away [the lower],
Enter the teachings of the Buddha.
Just like an elephant atop a reed hut,
Destroy the Lord of Death.

One who very mindfully
Transforms actions within the discipline of Dharma
Will thoroughly abandon the wheel of birth,
Causing suffering to end. [73]

Once one has fully contemplated the factors that place and keep us in this cycle of suffering, a strong wish for freedom will arise. Such a constant wish will make you a practitioner of the Medium Scope. When this motivation becomes the basis for developing the aspiration to become fully enlightened for the sake of all beings, it is called "a path in common," meaning that it is a path shared by persons of the Great Scope. Having gained true renunciation, there are three superior trainings that the Buddha taught in order to gain liberation: ethical discipline, concentration, and wisdom. Ethical discipline cultivates a firm root for developing virtues and a steady mind. It also keeps you within higher realms of existence and weakens mental afflictions. Concentration pacifies the mind and suppresses the afflictions, allowing the mind to stay one-pointedly on its object while bringing body and mind into balance. With the basis of these first two trainings, wisdom can be fully developed. It is ultimately wisdom that liberates the mind. Gungthang Rinpoche states:

> *Pillars and beams, supporting struts, and cross-sectioning,*
> *Assembled make a lovely home.*
> *By assembling the three superior trainings,*
> *The excellent house of holy liberation is attained.*[74]

The Great Scope Stage

> *By the suffering of one's own continuum,*
> *Whoever truly wishes to thoroughly end*
> *All the sufferings of others,*
> *That being is supreme.*[75]
> *—Jowo Atisha*

At some point during the development of a healthy individual, a stage of full maturity can be reached in which one is not only capable of self-care and responsible for long-term goals, but one also becomes able to care for others. Similarly, by recognizing your own suffering and its causes, you can expand your awareness to recognize the suffering of others around you. Just like you, they want to be happy, but they are caught in the same cycle of suffering that ensnares you. Seeing their suffering as unnecessary and as removable can cause you to engender the compassion and courage to help them find freedom.

Such an attitude, *bodhicitta*,[76] is said to give rise to many benefits. It is the only entrance to the Great Vehicle[77] of Buddhism, the way of Bodhisattvas. By holding *bodhicitta* as your motivation for practice, you surpass practitioners with lower goals, who only seek their own well-being. Great virtue is easily accumulated while negative karma and mental afflictions are quickly removed. Your goals become easily attained and you are guarded from interferences and harm. You will become able to quickly complete the stages of the path and become a true unending source of happiness for all beings.

But how is one to give rise to true *bodhicitta*? In the beginning, it is important to cultivate equanimity for others because otherwise your feelings will be biased—cherishing friends and relatives while disregarding strangers and disliking those who trouble you. Such a partisan approach belies underlying feelings of attachment for those who benefit or attract you, anger towards those who annoy or harm you, and ignorant indifference towards everyone else. One technique for neutralizing such bias is to imagine your closest friend, your worst enemy and a stranger in front of you, noticing the feelings each engenders. Then ask yourself how your feelings might change should your friend betray you, or the enemy sincerely apologize for past transgressions after doing some great service for you and so forth. We can see how in this life friends can become enemies, enemies can become friends, and strangers can evolve into either category. How many more times has this happened through the beginningless cycle of our previous lives?

The Buddha said:

> *Unimaginable, Bhikkhus, is the beginning to the round of births.*
> *For beings obstructed by ignorance and fettered by craving,*
> *Migrating and going the round of births, a starting point is not evident.*
> *It is not easy, Bhikkhus, to find a being who has not formerly been one's mother...*
> *Been one's father...one's brother...sister...son...daughter during this long, long time.*[78]

In the Great Vehicle tenets of Buddhism, it is asserted that, in fact, every single sentient being has been your mother multiple times due to the sheer magnitude of rebirths you have taken. If you contemplate the kindness of your mother of this life—how she carried you in her womb as someone infinitely precious, avoided foods that might have harmed you, risked her life in the agony of childbirth, forsook all her own comforts to provide you with food/shelter/companionship, cleaned you, taught you how to walk/talk/survive and so on—it is clear that you owe her a great debt. But also, every being, in the infinite regress of your past lives, has provided similar care. By contemplating this deeply, a genuine gratitude can be generated—a profound wish to repay the kindness of all beings and relieve their suffering. If your mother was blind and insane, stumbling towards a precipice, and you, her child, were there to rescue her, of course you would guide her to safety. Similarly, your mothers from infinite past lives are now blinded by ignorance, insane due to their mental afflictions, and stumbling towards the precipice of lower births. If we, their children, will not help them, then who will? Gungthang Rinpoche says to this:

> *Moreover, it is wrong to forsake old mother beings*
> *And then pursue your own benefit.*
> *Abandoning all his loved ones on an island in the sea*
> *Is not a ship captain's way of conduct.*[79]

Though our bodies, status, races, genders and so forth may be different, we are all equal in that we wish to be happy and do not want to suffer. It is the selfish clinging to one's own well-being that strengthens the mental afflictions and leads to the accumulation of negative karma causing suffering. In fact, it is the self-cherishing mind—rooted in ignorance—that constitutes the main obstacle to the Bodhisattva's path. We can see how selfish people eventually come to misery, social isolation, and despair, even in this life. Through the course of our infinite past lifetimes, according to the scriptures, self-cherishing has been the primary source of every imaginable woe we have encountered. Therefore, Bodhisattvas ask themselves, "If my selfish mind was ever to make me happy, wouldn't it have done so by now?" Shantideva says:

> *Throughout countless eons*
> *You have sought your own ends,*
> *And through such great effort*
> *You've achieved only suffering.*[80]

In contrast, if we look at the unshakable happiness of the awakened ones,[81] they have gained it from cultivating the mind of cherishing others. Compassionate people tend to be well-loved, supported and successful. This trend continues in the form of happy migrations in their future lifetimes due to the positive karma they accrue in helping others. To this, Shantideva states:

All those who are happy in the world
Are so because they want happiness for others.[82]

Realizing this, Bodhisattvas make a definite decision to exchange their old habit of primarily cherishing themselves with a new resolve to primarily cherish others and work for the benefit of all sentient beings. In order to facilitate and enhance this motivation, they secretly undertake the practice of "giving and taking." Giving practice is based on cultivating genuine loving-kindness for all beings, wishing that all beings encounter only happiness and its causes. Taking practice is based on intense compassion, wishing for all beings to be separated from suffering and its causes. In the beginning, Bodhisattvas imagine inhaling their own suffering that will befall them in the future and use that imagined suffering to reduce and eliminate their own selfish habits. Then, with a sense of kind concern for their own future selves, they imagine exhaling their own virtue as light bringing happiness and its causes to their future. After starting this way, they then imagine compassionately inhaling the sufferings of others in a similar fashion, and with loving kindness, imagine breathing out virtues in the form of light taking the aspect of whatever is needed to promote the temporal and ultimate happiness of others. Eventually, they extend this practice to every being, everywhere, continually imagining giving and taking with every breath.

While such practices are quite effective in reducing selfishness and in enhancing love and compassion, they have little direct impact on the immediate situations distressing beings. This realization leads Bodhisattvas to develop the extraordinary wish to actually take upon themselves the burden of liberating all beings. This dedicated resolve to bring all beings to freedom is conjoined with the insight realizing that, in order to accomplish such a goal, one must fully develop one's capacity to help others. Only a fully enlightened being has completely removed obstacles to suffering and to knowledge. Only a fully enlightened being has consummated the development of compassion, enlightened activities, and skillful means necessary to bring full benefit to others. Therefore, thinking in this way, the Bodhisattva gives birth to *bodhicitta*, the mind intent on enlightenment in order to liberate all beings from suffering. When such a motivation, through repeated cultivation, becomes genuine and spontaneous, all the virtuous activities of that Bodhisattva produce an unusually potent form of merit capable of continually ripening beneficially, culminating in one's ultimate goal. Gungthang Rinpoche says:

Once the fruit of other trees is taken, it is finished;
The wish-granting tree's fruit is without end.
Once the fruit of other virtues is enjoyed, it is finished;
The virtues of bodhicitta continually increase.[83]

In order to maintain and enhance the precious motive of *bodhicitta*, it is important to reflect on its benefits day after day. It should be generated at least six times each day as one tries to dedicate all one's activities to the benefit of beings, never abandoning the intent to help them, and continually developing one's own virtues and wisdom. These practices will keep you on the Great Vehicle path during this lifetime. In order to help you preserve the attitude of *bodhicitta* throughout future lives, it is taught that you must abandon all forms of deception, be honest with your teachers and beings, and never cause someone to regret a virtue. It is also important to praise Bodhisattvas while seeing them as enlightened and holding them as your guides.

There are two levels of *bodhicitta*, aspirational and engaged. At the aspirational level, one's wish to become enlightened for the benefit of others remains as merely a motivation. It is a bit like wishing to go on a trip to some new place. At the engaged level, one actually takes up the vows and practices of a Bodhisattva. This is like actually setting out on one's journey. The path one takes is called the "perfection vehicle," which has six practices beginning with the perfection of generosity. Je Tsongkapa states:

Generosity is the wish-granting gem, fulfilling the hopes of beings.
It is the supreme weapon to cut the knot of miserliness,
The Bodhisattva activity that generates unshrinking courage,
And the foundation for your good reputation to be proclaimed in the ten directions.
Knowing this, the wise pursue the excellent path of completely giving away
Body, wealth and virtue.
I the yogi have practiced this way,
You who seek liberation should do likewise.[84]

One perfects generosity by completely overcoming stinginess and developing an unrelenting intention to give everything to others. We eventually will have to give away our wealth, estates and bodies when death forces it upon us, therefore the Bodhisattva simply makes the resolve to do so now. In order to perfect this practice, one needs the basis of *bodhicitta* as one's motivation, and attempt to give appropriately while keeping in mind the other perfections. It is important not to regret one's acts of generosity, and therefore, it is wise to start with small things, gradually progressing to giving more valuable gifts. Much can be said about this practice, but briefly, Gungthang Rinpoche states:

> *Bodhisattvas give away all their wealth*
> *And the fruit of their virtues: it is supreme generosity.*
> *The rain nourishes all vegetation and crops*
> *But has no hope of repayment.[85]*

The second perfection is concerned with ethical discipline, which constitutes refraining from harming others in thought and deed. There are three levels of Bodhisattva morality: refraining from wrongdoing through the vows of individual liberation, collecting virtue through practicing the six perfections, and benefiting others through actual direct activities intended to remove their suffering and bring them well-being. According to Je Tsongkapa:

> *Morality is water cleansing the stains of negative actions,*
> *Cooling moonlight to dispel the tormenting heat of the delusions,*
> *Like the majestic king of mountains in the midst of beings.*
> *By its power, without coercion, all beings bow down.[86]*

Patience is the third perfection and its practice constitutes letting go of harms done to you, accepting the suffering that comes to you, and maintaining your trust and adherence to the path even through difficult times. Many avenues of analysis can be used to undermine rationalizing anger and hostility, but in brief, Shantideva writes:

Why be unhappy about something
If it can be remedied?
And what is the use of being unhappy about something
If it cannot be remedied?[87]

Like armor, patience protects the Bodhisattva from the mental afflictions that arise when confronted with life's inevitable hardships. It keeps the mind happy and uplifted, undisturbed by the burning fires of hatred. You become unruffled by the abuses of others, making you a calm eye in the storm of existence. Medical research is discovering health risks, including heart disease, are associated with high levels of stress and anger. Therefore, patience helps your health and in the wider scope, patience also protects you from other sources of harm. As Gungthang Rinpoche points out:

Returning a thorn's prick
With a blow of your fist is a cause of derision.
Returning anger to one who harms you
Is cause only for your own ruin.[88]

All of the perfections are enhanced through the practice of effort, the fourth perfection. Perfecting effort leads to perseverance in facing hardships on the path, joy in developing virtues, and enthusiasm in aiding others. It helps you overcome sluggishness and procrastination, wasting time on meaningless activities, and giving in to discouragement. With effort you become more energized and confident in your practice. Gradually, your course on the path becomes steady like a large flowing river, your progress and realizations increase like a swelling lake, and just as all waters flow into the ocean, you can eventually bring all of your activities to successful completion. As Gungthang Rinpoche says:

> *If you do not let go of continuous, strong effort,*
> *There are no activities that cannot be accomplished.*
> *Look at how water drops, constantly falling,*
> *Make a hole in a rock mountain.*[89]

Meditation is the fifth perfection. As before, meditative equipoise is practiced in conjunction with the other perfections. In particular, meditation is linked together with the perfection of wisdom. Like a lantern-glass that guards a candle flame from being blown out by the wind, meditative stabilization protects the flame of wisdom, so that it may burn brightly, revealing its true nature. Je Tsongkapa says:

> *Meditative concentration is the king ruling the mind.*
> *When set, it is immovable like the lord of mountains.*
> *When directed, it engages all virtuous objects*
> *And brings the great bliss of a supple body and mind.*[90]

One can alter the object of focus for meditation based on one's personal need. For example, when feeling desire, you can focus on the unattractive aspects of the desired object. When feeling anger, focus on loving kindness, which pacifies anger. Contemplating dependent origination eliminates ignorance, investigating the constituents of your body and mind can reduce pride, and settling your mind on the inhalation and exhalation of your breath can free the mind from scattering and distraction. When feeling depressed, it is good to dwell on uplifting aspects of the path like one's perfect human life and potential for enlightenment. One can also visualize light. When overly giddy, reflecting on impermanence, the truth of suffering and so forth can ground you. There are also practices of focusing on the forms of enlightened beings, which have many benefits. However, the highest object of meditation is the ultimate nature of reality. To this, Je Tsongkapa writes:

Wisdom is the eye to see profound thusness,
The path destroying samsara's root,
The treasury of good qualities praised in all the scriptures,
Renowned as the supreme lamp dispelling the darkness of
ignorance.[91]

In the beginning, it is good to set a quiet place for formal practice and reduce one's activities. By practicing contentment and strong ethical discipline, you can simplify your life and start to direct increasing amounts of time and energy to your meditation practice. There are internal obstacles to practice including laziness, mental dullness, scattering of one's attention, and so forth, which can gradually be overcome through faith in your practice, continued effort, recollection, vigilance and the other remedies to distraction. These, along with the stages of meditation, should be learned from a qualified instructor. Gungthang Rinpoche says:

In the clarity of concentration, free from sinking and
excitement,
All good qualities appear.
In a lake, pure like a polished mirror of Bendurya,
Whatever reflects is clear.[92]

While sustaining the clarity and serenity of one-pointed concentration, you can then use your mind to investigate concepts that cling to notions of self-existence and develop wisdom, the sixth perfection. It is important to first identify this internal enemy of such concepts of self-existence, which are the source of every afflicted mental state, the very root of cyclic existence. Gungthang Rinpoche states:

> *To think, "I am," about the basis of designation—*
> *The collection of the heaps, and so forth—is mistaken.*
> *Though a great river seems a primal flow,*
> *It is the convergence of many lesser streams.*[93]

In other words, we grasp at a sense of "I" as if it were an independent, singular, permanent entity existing from its own side, but as we investigate it under analysis we find that no such self-existent "I" exists. Instead, if we investigate this sense of self, we find that its appearance arises in dependence on our psycho-physical constituents in conjunction with our mental-labeling process. Therefore, it is without essence. Gungthang Rinpoche remarks:

> *If analyzed by logic, a labeled object*
> *Has no established nature at all.*
> *A river drawn into a hundred small channels*
> *Leaves not even a drop of a trace.*[94]

Rather than contradicting the Buddha's teachings on karma, this realization in fact leads to a deeper understanding of how dependent origination and emptiness support each other. By understanding that all conditioned phenomena depend on cause and effect, we arrive at the correct understanding that objects lack an independent nature. Also, it is because phenomena lack self-existence that they can be transformed by cause and effect. For example, if a seed had a permanent, independent nature, it would always be a seed and would never be able to transform into a sprout. But, because it is empty—lacking an independent, self-nature—when the proper conditions of soil, warmth and moisture come together with the seed, it transforms into a sprout, losing the former nature of having been a seed.

The same holds true of our bodies and minds. Though we have bothe a learned as well as an innately ingrained sense of having a self, in reality our identities change based on the workings of karma as we move through life and death. Just as the seed transforms into a sprout based on the conditions of warmth, soil and moisture, we transform from one form of life into another based on our empty nature and the subtle workings of karma. The Fourth Panchen Lama, Losang Chokyi Gyeltsen writes:

> *Outer and inner phenomena are just like an illusion,*
> *A dream, a reflection of the moon in a clear lake.*

Bless me to realize that, though they appear, it is in an untrue manner,
And to complete concentration on illusoriness.

Cyclic existence and Nirvana lack even an atom of self-nature;
Cause and effect, dependent origination, are infallible;
These two are non-contradictory, arising in support of each other;
Bless me to realize this meaning of Nagarjuna's thought.[95]

It is this cooperative play between emptiness of self and the infallible workings of cause and effect that brings the Bodhisattva certainty about his or her capacity to become enlightened. Due to its lack of self-nature, the mind can transform into the enlightened state if the causal forces of the path are diligently cultivated. By accumulating sufficient virtue and wisdom, the seeds of a person's body and mind can eventually transform into the body and mind of a Buddha.

As you perfect the union of meditative concentration conjoined with the wisdom analyzing selflessness, you begin the process of dismantling the negative mental states formed on the basis of self-clinging which is the cause of your suffering. With continued effort over a long period of time, eventually the mental afflictions can be completely eliminated along with obstacles to knowledge. Doing so culminates in full enlightenment, at which point one can be of ultimate benefit to others by showing them the path to freedom.

Finally, once you are well trained in the above stages of the path, it is appropriate to enter the secret teachings of Buddhism, which rely on a close relationship with a fully qualified teacher. The Bodhisattva undertakes this quicker approach in conjunction with the other stages of the path in order to speed up the process of enlightenment. This is not done for selfish reasons, but because the Bodhisattva realizes that delaying enlightenment delays his or her ability to fully help others. Gungthang Rinpoche mentions:

> *The Cause Vehicle's path is long,*
> *But through Secret Mantra's means, you travel quickly.*
> *A great ship, difficult to draw across a plain,*
> *Moves as soon as it enters the ocean.*[96]

It is said that a proper understanding of these stages of the path ensures your future enlightenment. With practice, their truths will reveal themselves in your daily experiences and everything you encounter will dawn as reminders of the path. Gungthang Rinpoche's poems are stunning examples of this ability to foster awakening by using everyday observations of the natural world.

The Well-Spoken Water Shastra, Two Systems with a Rosary of Waves

1

Knowledge extending beyond the depth and horizon[97] of
    perception,
Filled with compassion's wish-granting jewels,
A crashing rosary of waves of enlightened activities,
Lord Buddha's Dharma ocean reigns victorious.

2

Just like a clear stream of water, free from murk,
Soothes the tormenting thirst of beings,
This fresh nectar of well-spoken advice
Will make the wise sigh with relief.

3

For offering, washing feet, dispelling evil and the like,
Pure, fragrant water,
Is good however it is used.
Just so, this well-spoken advice is of benefit to all.

4

By understanding the two systems of what to embrace and
    what to abandon,
Temporary and ultimate ends will be achieved,
Like a merchant, who, knowing all the signs
Fares into the ocean.

Secular Ethics

5

How can a person unable to ford a stream
Swim the ocean?
How can a person who does not understand basic decency
Comprehend the system of the Dharma?

6

One with unbiased intelligence,
Will absorb the good qualities of others.
The gently flowing brook gathers flowers
As it murmurs through the pure meadowlands.

7

Should an evil person wander to the ends of the earth,
He will collect only faults and vice.
It is the same as water that erodes a ravine,
Drawing along muddy debris.

8

At first, it's difficult to learn good qualities;
If you are not mindful, they will easily degenerate.
It is difficult to fill a vessel with droplets of water;
If the vessel spills, all is lost at once.

9

If you are able to bear the burden of austerities,
Other activities are not difficult.
If you have already gone into the water,
The rain will cause you no extra harm.

10

If you do not give up continuous effort, striving gradually,
Anything can be achieved.
A river slowly descends, surrounds a vast and huge region,
And then moves on.

11

Great works are slowly accomplished;
You won't reach the end by a rush of effort.
Though a great river moves slowly, it travels a long distance;
A wave might be powerful, but it won't go far.

12

If an activity you are considering is beyond your ability,
It is not right to do it even should someone urge you.
If you don't know how to swim,
Though urged by others, why jump into the water?

13

A river is a shared water offering;
The sun and moon are shared lamps.
A holy person is a shared crowning jewel,
And the holy Dharma is shared nectar.

14

A ship with large sails is the ocean's ornament;
An unclouded moon is the ornament of the sky;
A learned person is an ornament to the teachings;
A hero leading troops is the army's ornament.

15

When leaders and followers are noble and skillful in
        conduct,
Their mutual well-being is promoted and increased.
By the turning of their tides, one with the other,
The great ocean and rivers become friends.

16

A bad master and a bad servant,
Both cause each other to degenerate.
If water is poured into an unfired clay pot,
Both go to waste and ruin.

17

When many with a pretense of knowledge wield great
    power,
A country is led to destruction.
When water rises on every side,
A house cannot stand its ground.

18

When leaders and people are in harmony,
Enemies will have difficulty conquering them; not so if
    they are divided.
A river might be difficult to cross for a horse,
But if separated into many streams, even a sheep can cross.

19

A Dharma King collects taxes,
But with them, cares for his people.
Great clouds draw up the ocean's water,
Which then falls slowly, nurturing the earth.

20

An evil king may steal all his people's food and wealth,
But still, he is hungry and poor,
Like Mare-Faced Mountain,[98] which always blazes
Though constantly drinking the ocean's water.

21

Though you constantly pay a bad leader respect,
By merely failing to bribe him, he is angered.
Though you may boil water all day long,
Once taken from the fire, it cools.

22

No one likes an official
Who is arrogant and extremely cruel.
Even fish and the like won't stay
In violently turbulent waters.

23

All people naturally gather around
One who is compassionate and able to help.
All beings will resort to the shore
Of an ocean filled with jewels.

24

Rising to the heights, you may gain glory,
But from that, more fear arises.
The ocean is the source of jewels
And also the city of the savage Nadra.[99]

25

Trusting unknown persons as new companions
Becomes a cause for ruin.
Even the Bodhisattvas, leaders of geese,
Were snared and captured, resorting on a new lake.[100]

26

It doesn't take long to divide
Thin-eared[101] friends with gossip.
When mixed, water and milk are of one taste,
But they are parted by a goose's bill.

27

One who is wise discerns truth from falsehood,
While the foolish run after whatever is said.
The sound of a splash in water
Scatters most beasts of prey and other wild animals.[102]

28

When in their company, by the waxing and waning of
    good actions,
You can know if friends are virtuous or bad.
Though it is the same in being cool and clear, by its benefit
    or harm,
Recognize water as medicinal or poisonous.

29

Compared to a bad friend with an enticing, white smile,
A loving friend with a wrathful scowl is beautiful.
Drought-bearing clouds are white, but
Water-laden, black clouds are the farmer's elixir.

30

Someone thoughtful and good-natured is relied upon by
    all:
The highest, the lowest, and those in-between.
A bathing pool that is easily accessed
Is entered happily by everyone.

31

Arrogant persons acting crudely
Are hated as enemies, even by those unprovoked.
Annoyed with her proud, wanton display,
Dzahu drank the Ganga[103] in one gulp.

32

One who lords himself over the humble
Will fall into a dreadful abyss.
A fish swims proudly in the water,
But if washed up on dry land, it will die.

33

A bad-natured person may have only a little wealth
But arrogantly holds himself like a king.
A stream in a narrow canyon
Roars like an ocean's wave.

34

Not having seen the vast kingdom,
A fool in a remote place regards himself as great.
The turtle, proud of his well water,
Died at hearing stories of the ocean.[104]

35

The simple-minded are easily gladdened,
And the instant pleased, are also easily angered.
A stream, a short distance from its source,
Rises and sinks in a flash.

36

Should you take loving care of one who is ill-natured,
They will not notice your kindness, and will disturb you.
Though you pour cool water onto liquid rock,[105]
It will boil and burn more intensely.

37

You may harm a holy being,
Yet unangered, his patience keeps him at ease.
Water blessed with a cooking mantra,[106]
Though boiling when poured, becomes cool.

38

Benefit those without piety,
And once the deed is done, they will forget.
Having crossed to the far side of a river,
A boat, no longer needed, is discarded.

39

By the deeds of evil people individually,
Even a great country will be brought to ruin.
It is said that the leap of an evil Siddha
Split the Sita River into a hundred branches.[107]

40

Those beaten down by cruel people
Will not trust even the Holy Ones.
A goose, deceived by the moon's reflection in water,
Does not eat lotus roots even in the daytime.[108]

41

Although you correct a bad person,
When conditions are met, their faults will show.
A river diverted by a levee
Will follow its old course in times of flood.

42

Whether high or low, rich or poor, and so on,
A holy person's nature won't change.
Though a river be cool or hot,
Still, how could it lose its liquid nature?

43

Mischievous people, through advice
Followed by consequences, are easily subdued.
To clean dirty clothes, use clean water
And then good cleanser.

44

A person's inner faults and good qualities
Can be discerned through their actions;
Just as water is shown by circling waterfowl
And fire is known by smoke.

45

It is easy to see the faults and good qualities of others
But hard to witness your own behavior.
In a lake, the moon and stars of the sky all reflect clearly,
While its own depths are not seen.

46

Acting with bad intent and deceit
Might seem successful, but ends in ruin.
A river meanders forward
But descends lower and lower as it goes.

47

A sign of the end of a family lineage is the birth of a bad son.
A sign that virtue is exhausted is when bad thoughts arise.
A sign of one's own decline is the scattering of one's thoughts.
A sign of a spring running dry is the coming forth of many
     impurities.

48

A fool might accomplish something amazing through hard
    effort,
But a crafty person will steal away the fame.
Though a lotus might be born from a mountain,
The fame of its generation is taken by the water.[109]

49

One may not have knowledge from scripture or realization,
Yet be renowned as holy by deceived people.
It is like the thunderous sound of drought-bearing clouds
Devoid of nourishing seasonal rain.

50

In the dregs of time, "the self-arisen all-knowing ones"[110]
Can prove more dull than common folk during their
    training.
Water from a spontaneously born geyser might emerge hot,
But put to heat, it takes longer than cold water to boil.

51

A loud, untamed preacher
Whose mind is worse than a butcher
Is like the winter mist–
When it gathers in the valleys, it is especially cold.

52

Though a holy person may become poor
He will not perform acts contrary to the Dharma.
Though a swallow wanting rain might thirst,
It won't drink water that has fallen to the ground.

53

Wishing to make efforts at practicing virtue,
It is contradictory to acquire wrong livelihood.
If you want to grow flowers,
Will it help to pour hot water on them?

54

Should a great being decline for a while,
Later on, his magnificence will increase.
A lake sheathed in ice
Will gradually surge forth in spring.

55

Though a man of weak intelligence and zeal
Wins some prosperity, it will soon be lost.
A small pond whose water is cut off
Will soon dry up.

56

Without wealth, but wanting fine clothes and food,
Unstudied in the scriptures, but bearing a scholar's
    responsibilities,
Not knowing how to swim, yet crossing a lake;
Knowingly, you buy your own suffering.

57

It is improper to generate vast ambitions for wealth
Which exceed the measure of your virtues.
If a small lake or well swells beyond its limit,
It will spill over.

58

When some great and high achievement fails to come,
One begins engaging in methods and supplication rites.
If a levee is not already built,
It is difficult to channel water once it starts to rise.

59

Boldly proceeding with meaningless endeavors,
You ruin yourself and are not heroic.
It is like the lion, who died
By jumping at his reflection in the water.[111]

60

Though you wish to tame an enemy,
Your behavior should be unhurried and smooth.
Look at the water bird moving stealthily
To catch fish and other such things.

61

As you jealously hate another's wealth,
So will your virtues decline.
Jumping into a forceful river,
Only you die; it is not harmed.

62

Instead, if you want victory over enemies,
Put effort into attaining good qualities.
The way to cross a great river
Is to find a flat place and build a boat.

63

If you do not ruin your karma and virtue,
Enemies alone cannot overcome you.
The nature of a spring is not to dry up;
Even if covered with earth, it cannot be blocked.

64

Poverty and wealth, gain and loss, high and low,
All are arranged by your previous karmic acts.
From the churning of the water mandala
The mountains, continents, and outer wall evolved in
    stages.[112]

65

Most scholars become poor;
Fools are enriched with wealth.
Murky rivers teem
With frogs, tadpoles, and bugs.

66

From among a hundred, there is one hero.
From among a thousand, there is one scholar.
From Lake Madru comes "water gold."
From the great ocean comes jewels.

67

The unintelligent find wealth
But don't know how to use it.
Though a thirsty dog comes to a river,
He doesn't gulp, he licks.

68

Wealth that benefits neither you nor others
Is like having no riches.
Though a land is vast and wide, without water,
It is called a desert and abandoned by all.

69

You want to know how to increase your wealth,
But you need to know how to give a little away.
If you draw well water, it increases;
If left alone, it is dried up by sediment.

70

The foolish and ignorant may possess extensive wealth
But it will be no more than a cause of suffering.
The Seas of Enjoyment between the golden mountains[113]
Are always oppressed by thick darkness.

71

To keep wealth, you must amass merit;
If merit wanes, wealth easily declines.
A blooming tree might have abundant boughs,
But without water, it will dry up.

72

The power of merit and a virtuous mind
Mutually cause each other. What fortune!
Water's rain and rain's water
Alternately increase each other, becoming friends.

73

Talk might be much or little,
Yet its effectiveness is known when taken in hand.
However wide or narrow the breadth of water,
You will know whether it is deep or not when you cross it.

74

The forger of a well-founded system is a scholar;
His lead is easy to follow.
After a well-bred stallion finds a safe ford through water,
Even a dog will follow.

75

A sage treats everyone equally
Whereas one with biased eyes has great desire and anger.
It is easy to carry a full vase,
But one partially full sloshes heavily to and fro.

76

One whose every thought rises to his mouth
Is derided by all as untrustworthy.
Even children can cross
A descending, babbling stream.

77

A person who speaks little, smiles, and is precisely to the point
Is treated considerately by everyone.
Running silently and slowly,
A deep, wide river is difficult to fathom.

78

Like drawings in water,
Abandon negative thoughts immediately.
Make your virtuous commitments unshakeable,
Just like drawings in stone.

79

With good intentions, even worldly activities
All turn into Dharma.
By relying on a water wheel,[114] water from far below
Travels to the top of a very high mountain.

The Stages of the Path to Enlightenment

80

Mainly, if you give trust from the depths of your mind
To cause and effect and the Supreme Jewels, you will
    accomplish whatever you wish.
When the King of Deities sends rain,
Bountiful crops will arise.

81

Having finished the phase of wandering
In the valley of worldly Brahma's locks,[115]
In order to wash the stains of the two obstacles,[116]
Come to the path of the Holy Dharma.

82

Just as one reaches the glacial spring as the source
Of the best among the seven types of water,[117]
Dharma, free of deception and unmistaken,
Must come from the Victor's speech.[118]

83

From there, descending in stages, come the three paths[119]
Of the profound and vast practices,
Complete and unerring instructions,
Like a water offering to the fortunate one, Completely
    Awakened.[120]

84

Yet, in the time of great degeneration,
Lama Manjugosha[121] made things clear,
Like the fish's form pulling forth the four Vedas
Sinking in the ocean.[122]

85

Meeting with such teachings as these,
Who would enter mistaken paths?
Near the divine river Ganges,
Who would dig a saltwater well?

86

Those of small intelligence and little fortune,
Deceived by those rumored to be profound and deep, go
      the wrong way.
A deer, mistaking a mirage for water,
Experiences needless suffering.

87

Entering into Dharma's path,
First, rely upon a virtuous spiritual guide.
The foremost preparation for one wishing to go to sea
Is to seek out a skillful captain.

88

The Lama is the root of virtue and goodness
Of the world and that which is beyond it.
All the earth's trees, leaves and fruit
Are the kindness of the naga dwelling in Lake Madru.[123]

89

By abandoning pride, being peaceful and subdued,
Become a fit vessel for the Holy Dharma.
Water cannot stay on a hilltop;
It pools into a low valley.

90

All Dharma cannot be grasped at once,
Yet however much is known will be of benefit.
You can't gulp down a whole river,
But whatever is drunk dispels thirst.

91

If you listen much, but do not practice
There is no benefit for your mind.
Staying in water for a hundred years,
A stone's nature is to remain dry.

92

Just as the stages of swimming with an empty skin bag[124]
Are always grasping it, sometimes grasping it, and not
    grasping it,
When listening to, contemplating, and meditating on
    general meanings,[125]
The mode of dependence is said to be three.

93

In the boat of a human life found at this time,
Relying on the sails of listening, contemplation, and
    meditation,
You can cross over the ocean of existence.
Later, this vessel will be hard to find.

94

Though the doorways to the six types of birth[126] are vast,
The complete eight leisures are very rare.
Though countless rivers flow,
Just a few have the eight qualities.[127]

95

From the very moment of birth, not abiding,
You head toward the mouth of the Lord of Death,
Just like a stream, which in each moment,
Flows irreversibly into the sea.

96

While grasped by the flesh-eater of impermanence,
In his teeth, how can you rest at ease?
When caught between the fangs of a water monster,
There is never an occasion for happiness.

97

Though accomplished, their end is never reached—
Forcefully cut worldly affairs.
Ripples on water press one on the other;
However much they chase, they never catch up.

98

You have power of mind and great versatility,
Yet are helplessly bound by the messenger of time.
The skilled dancer of a great lake's waves
In winter-time is trapped beneath the ice.

99

By non-virtuous actions through your three doors[128]
Future lives will definitely go to bad destinies.
Water descending from a mountain's peak[129]
Cascading, falls streaming into a ravine.

100

Then, for a billion years,
You'll burn and roast, but be unable to die.
A torrent of rain falls on a volcano,
To boil for an eon.

101

The sheltering refuge from those great fears
Is none other than the infallible supreme Three Gems.[130]
Carried by a river's current,
Only a boatman is sure to save you.

102

The blessings of the Supreme Three are boundless
But lacking faith—just so a protector.
The ocean is vast but cannot quench
The thirst of the rain-waiting sparrow.

103

Don't rely on one who is worldly,
Who hasn't crossed the swamp of cyclic existence.
If one borne off by water grabs another borne off by water,
Both will sink.

104

If you seek out the Supreme Three, practice with zeal
Their precepts on karma and its effects, what to accept and
    reject.
Though you rely on a captain,
If you do not stay in the boat, how will you be delivered?

105

All appearances of joy and sorrow of beings and their realms
Unerringly arise from karma gathered before.
It is said that though a water bowl is full,
It appears differently to the four types of beings.[131]

106

Collecting small virtues and non-virtues,
Your mind becomes full.
Amassing drops of rain
Forms even the vast water mandala.[132]

107

For now, something appears as a virtue,
But in your dedication and wish, there are many
    corruptions.
The supremely sweet water of the Ganges
Becomes bitter when mixed with the ocean.

108

Those blinded by the black murk of ignorance
And bound by the noose of karma,
Completely swept off by the river of craving existence,
Go to the ocean of miserable births.

109

Desire is a salty river,
No matter how much you drink, your thirst is never
    quenched.
Like a goose iced on a lake,
Rouse the sorrow wanting sure escape from samsara.

110

The sharks of karma and affliction
Infest the ocean of the cycle of suffering.
Free yourself; taking the great ship of the three trainings,[133]
Travel to the isle of liberation.

111

Don't taint specially vowed morality
With the stains of misdeeds and downfalls.
As when the ocean could not abide the corpse,[134]
Guard your vows with firm recollection and alertness.

112

Moreover, it is wrong to forsake old mother beings
And then pursue your own benefit.
Abandoning all his loved ones on an island in the sea
Is not a ship captain's way of conduct.

113

Abiding in a lake, wavering, and unreality
Are the three aspects of the moon in water.
The three kinds of compassion for beings are similar.[135]
By them, plant the life-root of the Great Vehicle.

114

Virtue influenced by *bodhicitta* is endless,
Becoming a cause to go to the great enlightenment.
Because the fruit of the *jambu* [136] falls into Lake Madru,
It becomes the nature of pure gold. [137]

115

The activities of the Conquerors' sons are endless
Yet they are contained in the six perfections,
Just as a hundred streams flowing from mountain gorges,
    passes and valleys
Gather underneath one bridge.

116

Bodhisattvas give away all their wealth
And the fruit of their virtues: it is supreme generosity.
The rain nourishes all vegetation and crops
But has no hope of repayment.

117

Pure morality removes, without exception,
The mud of failings and transgressions.
Powder of the Ketaka's fruit[138]
Makes a murky river clear.

118

Patience conquers the enemy of hatred,
Which burns your accumulated virtues, leaving none.
Water is the lethal antidote
To the all-consuming tongue of a blazing fire.

119

If you do not let go of continuous, strong effort,
There are no activities that cannot be accomplished.
Look at how drops of water, constantly falling,
Make a hole in a rock mountain.

120

In the clarity of concentration, free from sinking and
   excitement,
All good qualities appear.
In a lake, pure like a polished mirror of *bendurya*,[139]
Whatever reflects is clear.

121

Seeing that all things are empty
Dispels all the suffering of samsara.
Agastya gulped down all the rivers.
Flowing out, they became nectar.[140]

122

Nagarjuna, with his ocean-vast mind,
Stole the confidence of those who speak of self-existent
   things.
The awesome, dark depths and expanse of the fathomless sea
Terrify the childish.

123

To analyze profound thusness,[141]
You must first be certain about the object of refutation.
To take gems from the ocean,
It is important to know where the dangers lie.

124

To think, "I am," about the basis of designation—
The collection of the heaps, and so forth—is mistaken.
Though a great river seems a primal flow,
It is the convergence of many lesser streams.

125

If analyzed by logic, a labeled object
Has no established nature at all.
A river drawn into a hundred small channels
Leaves not even a drop of a trace.

126

Whatever the Teacher taught,
Is included into this: emptiness and dependent arising.
Without exception, every river on earth
Flows and descends into the great ocean.

127

A bodhisattva whose mind is ripe
Nurtures disciples with the four ways of gathering.[142]
A captain experienced in navigating the sea
Leading others as well, brings them to wealth.

128

The Cause Vehicle's path is long,
But through Secret Mantra's means, you travel quickly.
A great ship, difficult to draw across a plain,
Moves as soon as it enters the ocean.

129

The Vajra-Holder elucidated well
This inconceivably potent Secret Mantra.
Even by uttering "suffering mother"
One summons the divine river.[143]

130

The non-dual state is the abode of the naga king.[144]
The first easy step to the entrance
Of the great ocean of the Vajra Vehicle
Is the staircase of the precious four empowerments.[145]

131

But, the pledges and vows are the basis
Upon which the two types of attainments[146] depend.
If the root of the ocean's water dries up,
From whence could the rosary of waves arise?

132

For a yogi knowing thusness,[147]
Though desire is used, there is no attachment.
Though a fish swims into the water's very depths,
It is unharmed by the water.

133

The faults of the mental afflictions, desire and so forth,
Are conquered by the path, itself made of mental affliction.
Water in the ear is removed by water,
A burn from fire is soothed by contact with fire.[148]

134

The subtle and rough yogas of the generation stage[149]
Purify birth, death and the intermediate state,
Just like Kelden Shingta's water offering[150]
Cleansed the poisonous stain.

135

The innate great bliss of the four joys[151]
Becomes the vast wisdom of the four emptinesses.[152]
The descent of the four river currents[153]
Makes the great fire of Mare-Faced Mountain blaze.[154]

136

From the subtle, primordial wind-mind,[155]
The illusion-like body arises,
Like a water-bubble from pure water
And a cloud from the clear sky.

137

As in each dew-drop on every blade of grass
The moon's reflection appears,
Each successive example
Can illustrate all phenomena of samsara and beyond.

138

From the manners of good-natured worldly folk
To the stages of the paths of Sutra and Mantra,
This one example that illustrates them
Is the ocean of miraculous good explanation.

139

In the water treasury of the enjoyment-wheel,[156]
The singing swans play.
From their mouths come waves of excellent explanations
Swaying the vines.

May the new moon of whatever good explanation has been born from the water treasury of my mind, steal away the darkness of the world's ignorance and dispel the heart's sadness with its cool touch.

May its virtue be held by the excellent fabric of pure white light in the three worlds, and may intentions for good deeds in all beings' minds, together with the ocean of teachings, always increase.

The Well-Spoken Wood Shastra, Two Systems with a Hundred Branches

OM! May there be happiness and goodness.

1

I bow to the Buddha tree
With its firm root of the precious mind
And fully developed branches of the two collections of
    great activities,
Bent by clusters of the excellent fruit of the three bodies.[157]

2

Appearances arise for practitioners
As examples of many holy instructions.
On the floor of a dense forest,
Are endless heaps of leaves from trees.

3

If you rely upon a wish-granting tree,
All that you need and want comes down like rain.
Similarly, if you rely on a holy spiritual friend,
A mass of goodness is spontaneously achieved.

4

Those who disrespect their spiritual guide,
Though understanding a hundred scriptures, derive no
     benefit.
Throw dry wood into water for a hundred years,
Yet, it is impossible for it to sprout leaves and branches.

5

To one who is faithful and of good nature,
Merely a single verse will be of benefit.
A tree's new sprout
Grows even by a drop of rain.

6

Though thorny and poisonous plants are unwanted,
The world is full of them.
Beings with no leisure, gone to evil births,
Are countless, like the dust particles of the earth.

7

The white sandalwood tree
Just barely exists in this world.
This excellent body also, complete with leisure and fortune,
Having obtained the vast path, is just barely unhindered.

8

If the essence of this leisure and fortune is not taken,
It is no different from having taken an animal's birth.
If the mango fruit is not enjoyed,
What is its distinction from a castor oil plant?

9

Time changes even a single tree's complexion—
Its leaves, fruit, flowers and so forth.
The drama of birth, old age, sickness and death
Changes instant by instant.

10

Leaves joined to trees for a long time,
Once fallen, never come again.
Lovers who have stayed together for a long time,
Are one day separated forever.

11

By splitting, chopping, and sectioning a tree trunk
A lumberjack quickly becomes exhausted.
Karma may similarly be enacted for an eon,
Yet, the guardians of hell are not fatigued.

12

For as long as non-virtue is not finished,
Suffering will be experienced constantly.
As long as a poisonous seed remains,
It is natural that a poison leaf grows.

13

Whoever has gone for refuge to the Three[158]
Does not fall to samsara nor to a lesser peace.[159]
One who relies upon a great tree,
Cannot be harmed by fierce beasts of prey.

14

It is a sign of foolishness to rely
On a tree with rotten roots.
Alas! How mistaken are they who grasp as a refuge
Someone also sunk in samsara.

15

From poisonous and medicinal sprouts
There is never errant fruit.
From virtuous and non-virtuous deeds as well
The coming forth of some other fruition is impossible.

16

Karma collected from beginningless time,
Though a hundred eons pass, is never wasted.
The fruit of the Tala tree[160] might be withered for a
    thousand years,
Yet if touched by moisture, it will germinate.

17

When its small seed ripens, the Nyadrota's[161] branches and
 leaves
Grow to cover the distance traveled by a shout.
Even giving one bite of food
Results in attaining the status of a wheel-turning king.

18

The various aspects of this wheel of existence
Are without any meaning or essence.
A plantain tree's moist trunk
Is all, from tip to bottom, without pith.

19

A tree might live for a hundred years,
But sometime it will fall.
Even having gone to samsara's peak,[162]
Again, one will go to unbearable bad destinies.

20

If the sugar-cane's juice is spread well,
It is able to remove even the Tikta's[163] bitterness.
By cultivating well the truth of the path,
The root origin of suffering is abandoned.

21

Pillars and beams, supporting struts, and cross-sectioning,
Assembled make a lovely home.
By assembling the three superior trainings,[164]
The excellent house of holy liberation is attained.

22

The Dzendu's seed[165] was born from another.
Thus it is without beginning.
In births without limit in cyclic existence,
Who has not been your father and mother?

23

The heavy load of a hundred horses and oxen
Is delivered by one great wooden cart.
The burden that cannot be carried by all the Shravakas and
    Pratyekabuddhas[166]
Beautifies the shoulders of the Bodhisattva.

24

Once the fruit of other trees is taken, it is finished;
The wish-granting tree's[167] fruit is without end.
Once the fruit of other virtues is enjoyed, it is finished;
The virtues of *bodhicitta* continually increase.

25

Beings gather at a tree
Made beautiful by fully ripened fruit.
One without avarice, majestic in giving,
Satisfies the hopes of all kinds of beings.

26

The root of higher realms and definite goodness[168]
Is none other than morality.
The root of abundant boughs and leaves
Is only the trunk of a tree.

27

Returning a thorn's prick
With a blow of your fist is a cause of derision.
Returning anger to one who harms you
Is cause only for your own ruin.

28

If you do not give up effort at the time of the cause,
All good qualities will arise at the time of the result.
If a root is not separated from moisture,
Leaves and fruit will ripen at the top.

29

If a tree trunk is rocked by wind,
Its fruit will fall to the ground.
Similarly, concentration's object is lost when shaken
By sinking, scattering, and wandering.

30

From very pure meditative absorption
Come the good qualities of clairvoyance and the like.[169]
If a sapling does not deteriorate,
The heads of its flower stamens sway.

31

Brandishing a wooden sword on the battlefield
Causes merriment in your enemies.
False, partial views
Cause derision in those who long to cut samsara's root.

32

Fine white sandalwood
Dispels the suffering of fever.
Views imbued with compassion's essence
Tear from the roots the hundred illnesses of the three
      poisons.[170]

33

Wood-born bugs
Consume the wood.
Likewise, wisdom born from desire
Eliminates the faults of desire.

34

As white trees, soaked by moisture,
Are transformed into the color of *bendurya*,[171]
Likewise, ordinary appearances, made pure by Clear Light,
Arise as a pure deity's body.

35

A tree, replete with branches and leaves,
Cools all that its shadow covers.
A Buddha, complete and lacking no good quality,
Is the protector of every kind of being.[172]

Secular Ethics

36
Thus is the chapter from the Wood Shastra
On the path of Dharma.
Now I will tell you some verses on worldly manners.
Give heed and listen!

37
The dignity of a Dharma king
Brings even enemies under his influence.
The fragrance of the Malaya Born[173] is a messenger
Drawing in the bees.

38

A bad king, who oppresses his subjects:
At times even his servants will not come around.
Though you scatter a heap of peas with a cudgel,
They will never stick to the club's surface.

39

If disrespected by ministers and citizens,
How can a great king stand?
If a beam is not supported by a pillar,
From what will the king's palace rise?

40

The kindness of a good leader
Increases the influence of his retinue.
By relying on a great tree,
A vine's tip will reach the sky.

41

If you lean on a thorny plant,
It gives rise to the pain of pierced vital spots.
Likewise, relying on bad people,
Later produces only suffering.

42

An increase in the happiness of the citizens
Is a sign the leader himself is great.
Wide, fully developed branches
Are the beautiful ornament of the tree's trunk.

43

A leader's impoverished servants,
While he himself is wealthy, are a cause of shame.
No matter how wide a tree's trunk may be,
If it has no leaves and branches, it is naked.

44

One dwelling at the roots of a rotten trunk
Is always ill at ease, day and night.
A bad master's servants, too,
Are always worried, oppressed by anguish.

45

Though bad leaders' servants flee,
When a good leader expels them, they return.
A thorn plant repels bees,
But if chased from a mango tree, they swarm it again.

46

Though a leader, when new, is benevolent,
Later he imposes a burdensome tax.
Though you go to a tree for shelter from rain,
Afterwards, a heavy stream of drops falls.

47

A tree's shadow cools all equally.
The sun and moon's light illumines all equally.
A cloud's water rains on all equally.
A king's rules apply to all equally.

48

Although a master is good, if his attendants are bad,
It is difficult to approach and be near him.
Who would lean on a sandalwood tree
Wrapped round by a venomous snake?

49

It is said that there are four types of mango fruit—
Outwardly and inwardly ripe and unripe.
With people also, minds and actions both
Can be pure and impure, there are many types.

50

A scholar, having all good qualities,
Without conceit, is peaceful and subdued.
A plant's tip, laden with the burden
Of its grain, remains bent over.

51

A person with no good qualities
Has an exceptionally high state of pride.
The nature of a tree, holding no ripened fruit,
Is to be unbending.

52

If one has no innate good qualities,
What benefit is a pretense of outward manners?
Hang a diadem on a dry tree, barren of leaves and
    branches,
But what beauty is there?

53

For one who is distracted when at study and practice,
Wanting to be a scholar is a fruitless hope.
For a tree whose flowers are destroyed by frost,
There is no hope for fruit.

54

If someone is without intelligence,
High position is but a basis for shame.
A lion made from wood looks ferocious,
But has no heart.

55

If it has no sweet fragrance,
Though you say "this is sandalwood," you lie.
If not in accord with holy conduct,
To proclaim oneself a holy one is devoid of meaning.

56

Should a base person be elevated to kingly status,
Still, he will engage in corruption.
Even though a plantain tree is born upright,
Its leaves hang down.

57

Cut Agarwood[174] into a hundred pieces,
Yet its innate fragrance is not lost.
Similarly, however impoverished the holy become,
How would they ever abandon their good nature?

58

When leaves of a juniper tree are put into a fire,
Their fragrance expands even more.
Likewise, when harm is done to one with a noble mind,
Afterwards their greatness shows.

59

Although a pure person stays in retreat,
Their fame is proclaimed by the gods.
The fragrance of sandalwood,
Born from the southern mountain, is spread by the wind.

60

Though crooked wood can be straightened,
When it meets moisture, it becomes warped.
Though one with bad nature can be corrected,
When he meets with opportunity, his faults show.

61

A small-minded person with a bad character
Might have good qualities, but they are of no benefit.
A flower with roots set in poison
Might be beautiful, but who needs it?

62

Both juniper and sandalwood pillars
Have equal ability to hold up a beam.
If they have courage, both rich and poor
Are equal when set to a task.

63

Though people are equal in wealth and power,
Their goodness or evil is known by their actions.
Though equal in thickness, if thrown into water,
The heads and ends of pieces of wood can be discerned.

64

A wise person who journeys to another country
Will be valued and respected by all.
A tree born in a forest
Will do the work of wood in another place.

65

Cotton, blown away by the wind,
Not staying on mountain peaks, settles in the valleys.
A small-minded person wanders to the ends of the world[175]
And then finally falls into ruin.

66

It is very easy to become stained by faults;
Training in good qualities is not like that.
It is easy for a flame to spread to wood,
But hard to divide a river into streams.

67

If two corrupt people become companions,
Eventually both one and the other fail.
Rubbing two pieces of dry wood together
Ends with both being burnt.

68

Though a tree is fully developed,
If given too much water, its roots are destroyed.
An eminent person may have good qualities,
But a bad companion can bring him down.

69

Splicing two types of fruit trees together
Brings forth a third type of fruit.
If two intelligent people associate,
Unprecedented, good wisdom is born.

70

An elephant dwelling in the cool shadow of a tree,
Destroys the tree's roots.
Trusting in bad attendants
Will ruin the roots of good deeds.

71

The tree top supports the bird,
Who drops his feces when he goes.
If one takes a bad[176] spouse,
Some day he will leave a bad mark and then go.

72

However much you help a bad person,
There is no hope of him returning the benefit.
Though wood always nurtures the fire,
Fire turns it into ashes.

73

Even a single wise and powerful person
Will accomplish the needs of all, whether high or low.
Just a single bow made from wild bamboo
Works for a thousand arrows.

74

If you do not have enough wealth,
Even being upper class has little meaning.
When a tree does not provide the cool shade you need,
What is the benefit of its high crown?

75

If there are no roots of virtue,
Collecting things will not dispel poverty.
Why spread water on branches
When the trunk is lacking moisture?

76

You wish to increase wealth by interest on loans,
But the root savings are often destroyed.
Trees born in one place that are cut
And replanted in another, mostly dry up.

77

Similar to the fruit of a Sahakara tree[177]
Born on a high cliff,
Great wealth that does not benefit anyone,
Yourself or others, is a mere decoration.

78

The advice for those wishing to increase their wealth
Is to give a part of it away.
If you wish to develop the branches of a tree,
A good method is to cut the tips.

79

An inferior person collects, but does not accomplish.
A virtuous person gives, but becomes wealthy.
On moist ground, a tree will grow even if you cut it.
In a dry place, it will never grow even though you plant it.

80

The fruit of a tree on the side of a path
Causes a rain of children's stones to descend.
Likewise, the wealth of a bad owner
Is mostly the waving in of enemies.

81

Should wealth come to persons of lesser virtue,
They will lose even their lives.
Fruit growing on the tip of a bamboo tree
Is an omen of degeneration.

82

Sugar cane is cut for the sake of its taste.
A fox is killed on account of its skin.
Merchants gather for the purpose of wealth.
One opposes a bad king for the good of the people.

83

First draw a line on the wood,
Then cutting and sawing needs no correction.
You must think at the start of activities.
To regret afterward is the sign of a fool.

84

Who would boast of intelligence[178]
Though their success is just by good luck?
"A sleeping tree's leaves shrivel, therefore it has mind,"
This is the system of the errant.

85

Everyone tramples a tree whose branches and leaves
Are scattered at a crossroad.
A person who says many meaningless and confused things,
Is valued little by anyone.

86

When a bad person does even a small favor,
He will fill your ears, bragging of great kindness.
Though the fire is small, wet wood
Fills the kitchen with black smoke.

87

A tree which once was a snake's den
Causes fear when seen later on.
Suspicion always arises
About one who has stolen or lied just once.

88

Even a sharp thorn will break its tip
If it strikes a stone mountain.
If you criticize a holy person out of jealousy,
You will demean yourself.

89

In these dregs of time, if you are too humble
Towards one who is unworthy, all will deride you.
Cotton is called "So soft!"
Doesn't everyone use it as a cushion?

90

Wood that grows straight is beautiful,
But crooked wood is even better for a saddle.
It is good to have an upright character,
But the Buddha said to sometimes be flexible.

91

An arrow shot without its head
Is a messenger inviting the enemy.
If you do not have the power to conquer an adversary,
Why boast meaninglessly of conquest?

92

One loves a friend to excess,
But this often becomes a cause of resentment.
If you enjoy too much sweet sugarcane,
It turns into the sour belch of indigestion.

93

An ax is the enemy of trees,
Though its handle is made of wood.
A problem begun by an enemy,
Often has roots made by friends.

94

If you use a bad method to cut down a tree,
It will fall on you.
Excessive hatred of an enemy
Often leads to your own destruction.

95

A dry piece of wood you are unable to bend,
If soaked with moisture, becomes usable.
Though an enemy has an evil mind,
If you are skillful, you will be able to subdue him.

96

The flower of the sorrowless tree is not opened by the sun
  and moon.
It is opened by the touch of a young woman's anklet.[179]
Some ill-natured people, who don't listen though you
  explain things well,
Can be subdued by being put down.

97

Forest dwellers delight in a fine house,
And those who live in one, in a garden.
Lacking necessities, some go towards monkhood;
And those crazed by desire, towards a household.

98

Though a monkey is born in a forest,
It goes somewhere else when the fruit runs out.
When you are poor, even your dearly beloved child
Runs off to another place.

99

Above a bountiful forest, though uncompelled,
The birds of the sky will wheel.
To wherever the causes of happiness are complete,
Though not summoned, people will gather.

100

If a tree's fruit is well nurtured,
Leaves, branches and the rest will come by the way.
If you make efforts in the holy Dharma,
By that, worldly glory will also be achieved.

101

Thus are the two systems of what to accept and discard,
Using only the qualities of trees.
This endeavor of illustrative discourse
Is an unprecedented scholar's celebration.

102

In whose milk-ocean[180] throat
Swans[181] of poetry[182] frolic,
And from whose mouth come waves of well-spoken advice
Moving every type of vine,

103

By the jeweled lasso of whose fame
The edges of the earth of India and Tibet are tied,
Glorious Sakya Pandita, I have relied
On your path of well-spoken advice.[183]

104

The lock of these meanings is the width of a fist,[184]
While the key of these examples is as long as a forearm.
Though scriptures like this have appeared,
This one accords with both scholars and fools.

105

For those who wish to know the two systems of what to
    accept
And what to abandon, these examples are not merely a
    finger's width.
Look at the moon-face[185] of these meanings.
It has the wonderful sign of the rabbit.[186]

106

May the Nyadrota seed of this well-made effort
Ripen as a positive cause,
Extending its branches to the ten directions,
Accomplishing the benefit of all beings.

This poem, called *The Well-Spoken Wood Shastra, Two Systems with a Hundred Branches*, was composed upon seeing various phenomena. The Venerable Konchok Tenpai Dronme wrote it based on what he recalled from his travels along the path to the medicinal waters at Tsagen.

Acknowledgements

Many have helped to bring this work to completion. Particularly, we would like to thank John Cerullo, Casey Kemp and everyone at Karuna Publications for their work in preparing the text for publication. Clare Cerullo did an excellent job with the design, adding beauty and readibility to the text. Very special thanks go to Scott Bramlett, who spent countless hours pouring over the poems, editing out mistakes, helping with some of the endnote translations, and suggesting more poetic renderings of various portions of the texts. His invaluable help is deeply appreciated. Also, a dear friend and editor, Rick Finney, corrected several errors in the manuscript.

Tsewang Palmo input the Tibetan for Yeshe Khedrup's compilation of Gungthang Rinpoche's biography and also offered constant hospitality in her home as we worked on the translations. Sharon Hurley input the original Tibetan for both poems with the hope that a bilingual edition may eventually be published. Artemus Engle, one of the greatest living Western scholars of Tibetan Buddhism, offered constant support and many helpful suggestions. Roz Hurley and Steve Michalski also gave helpful feedback. We would also like to thank Susan Meinheit at the Library of Congress and the staff of Latse Library for helping us to find copies of the texts. In particular, deep thanks go to the late scholar, Gene Smith, for providing us a copy of Akya Yongdzin's commentary.

Finally, we apologize for any errors in these translations while rejoicing in any merit that may have accrued. If virtue has been created here, we dedicate it all to the long life of His Holiness the Dalai Lama, to the long lives of all true spiritual guides, and to the successful completion of all of their aspirations and endeavors. May all sentient beings be benefited and goodness increase!

Yeshe Khedrup and Wilson Hurley
November 2010

Endnotes

1   *Gung thang dkon mchog bstan pa'i sgron me* (1762-1823).

2   See "Songs of Spiritual Experience" by Thupten Jinpa and Jas Elsner, Shamabala Publications, Boston & London, 2000.

3   *Dhamma* (Sanskrit: *Dharma*) is a Pali word that refers ultimately to the realizations and cessations of awakened beings; and in a relative sense, to the teachings given regarding the path to the cessation of suffering (Pali: *Nibbana*) and to enlightenment.

4   Translated from the Pali by Bhikkhu Bodhi, *The Connected Discourses of the Buddha (A New Translation of the Samyutta Nikaya), Volume 1*, Wisdom Publications, Boston, 2000, page 284.

5   Ibid. page 285.

6   Quoted from *Elegant Sayings* by Nagarjuna and Sakya Pandita, Dharma Publishing, 1977.

7   Ibid.

8   The first in the line of Gungthang incarnations was the 50th Ganden Tripa, Gedun Puntsok (*dga' ldan khri pa dge 'dun phun tshogs*), who served as head of the Gelukpa order of Buddhism from 1715 to 1722. He took his name from Gungthang Monastery, located close to Lhasa, where he served as abbot.

9   Tib: *rab byung* (Sanskrit: *prabhava*). This term refers to sixty year cycles of the Tibetan calendar that begin in 1027 CE with the "Fire Hare Rabjung." It is an astrologically-based calendar.

10   *'Jam dbyangs bzhad pa dkon mchog 'jig med dbang po* (1728-1791).

11   *Dharma* is a Sanskrit word that means "to hold." In common
        usage it can refer to phenomena in general, but in this context
        it refers to the scriptural and realizational teachings of the
        Buddha. Here, the phrase "topics on Dharma practice" is a
        translation of the Tibetan phrase *chos sphod skor*, which is
        one of the names given to compilations of basic prayers and
        practices for daily recitation. Typically, young monks memorize
        such prayers and practices before beginning their studies of the
        Five Great Treatises.

12   These five root texts are the Pramanavartika Karika (Tib:
        Tsad ma rnam 'grel), Dharmakirti's text concerning logic; the
        Abhisamayalamkara (Tib: *mngon rtogs rgyan*), Maitreya's text
        on the perfection of wisdom; the Madhyamakāvatāra (Tib: *dbu
        ma 'jug pa*), Nagarjuna's composition on the middle way; the
        Abhidharmakosha (Tib: *mdzod rtsa ba*), Vasubhandu's text on
        Buddhist science; and the Vinaya Root Text (Sanskrit: *Vinaya
        mula sutra*; Tib: *mdo rtsa ba*), composed by Gunaprabha.

13   Sutras comprise the open discourses of the Buddha, and
        Tantras (synonyms include Secret Mantra, Vajrayana, and
        Result Vehicle) are the hidden, esoteric teachings of Buddhism.

14   A Bhikshu (Pali: Bhikkhu) is a fully ordained monk.

15   This title is awarded to the most accomplished Geshes at
        the monastic universities. The examination is in the form of
        debate, in which top scholars from the land challenge the
        aspirant's scriptural knowledge.

16   A Stupa is a reliquary mound symbolizing the path to
        enlightenment and the omniscience of the Buddha.

17   The Tibetan for these works, in order, is: *drang nges kyi mtshan,
        kun gzhi'i mtha' dpyod, bden pa bzhi'i rnam bshad, rten 'brel gyi
        mtha' dpyod.*

18   Tib: *rig byed ma'i bstod 'grel.*

19 The Tibetan for these texts, in order, is: *rje bla mar bstod pa don ldan gyi rang 'grel, chu dang shing gi bstan bcos, rgan byis 'bel gtam, 'jam dbyangs bzhad pa 'jigs med dbang po'i rnam thar, sde khri blo bzang don grub kyi rnam thar, thu'u kan chos kyi nyi ma'i rnam thar, sgo mang mkhan po chos dar gyi ram thar.*

20 Jampelyang is the name of Manjushri, the manifestation of the omniscient wisdom of the Buddhas.

21 Tib: *rgyal ba'i ring lugs pa chen po 'jam dbyangs bla ma dkon mchog bstan pa'i sgron me'i rnam par thar pa'i pad ma bzhad pa'i nyin byed.*

22 Lhasa Sholparma (*Lha sa Zhol dpar ma*) is the printing office in Lhasa located below the Potala Palace.

23 Verse five of the Water Shastra.

24 Verse 100 of the Wood Shastra.

25 B. Czeh, T. Michaelis, T. Watanabe, J. Frahm, G. de Biurrun, M. van Kampen, A. Bartolomucci, and E. Fuchs, "Stress-Induced Changes in Cerebral Metabolites, Hippocampal Volume, and Cell Proliferation Are Prevented by Antidepressant Treatment with Tianeprine," *Proceedings of the National Academy of Sciences of the United States of America* 98, 22 (2001): 12796-801. Cited from *Destructive Emotions, How Can We Overcome Them?* Bantam Books, 2003.

26 These and other mind-body research findings can be found in *Destructive Emotions, How Do We Overcome Them?*, narrated by Daniel Goleman, Bantam Books, 2003. See also, *Train Your Mind, Change Your Brain*, by Sharon Begley, Ballantine Books, New York, 2008.

27 *Pramanavarttikakarika,* quote drawn from Artemus Engle's book *The Inner Science of Buddhist Practice*, Snow Lion Publications, Ithaca, NY, 2009, Tsadra Foundation.

28 Ibid. See Artemus Engle's discussion of this, pp. 49-59, for a more detailed presentation of the subject.

29   Ian Stevenson MD et al, "With Written Records Made Before Verifications," University of Virginia Health Sciences Center, Charlottesville, VA 22908.

30   See Ian Stevenson MD, "Unlearned Language" and "Telepathic Impressions," University of Virginia Press.

31   From the Tibetan version of the *Dhammapada*: *chos rnams yid kyi rang bzhin te/yid ni gtso zhing sngon la 'gro/gal te gdug pa'i yid kyis ni/smras sam yang na byas kyang rung/de la de yis sduk bsngal 'thob/shing rta rjes su 'brang ba bzhin.//chos rnams yid kyi rang bzhin te/yid ni gtso zhing sngon la 'gro/gal te yid ni rab dvang pas/ smras sam yang na byas kyang rung/de la de yis bde ba 'thob/grib ma yol bar mi 'gyur bzhin.*

32   Stevenson, Ian, *Twenty Cases Suggestive of Reincarnation*, University of Virginia Press, 1974.

33   From the *Lalitavistara Sutra* as translated by Khenpo Kalsang Gyaltsan and Ani Kunga Chodron.

34   Ibid.

35   As translated by Thubten Jinpa.

36   From the *Mahaparinirvana Sutra* as translated by Khenpo Kalsang Gyaltsan and Ani Kunga Chodron.

37   Quoted from Je Tsongkapa's (*rje tshong kha pa blo bzang gvaqs pa*, 1357-1419) *Lam rim bsdus don ma: gzhung bzang stong gi chub o 'du ba*.

38   A Bodhisattva is a practitioner who aspires to become fully enlightened in order to be of supreme benefit to all sentient beings.

39   Voidness refers to the lack of self-nature of all phenomena.

40   Budhha's direct disciples Maitreya and Manjushri were divine, highest level Bodhisattvas, who then transmitted their lineage instructions to their respective earthly disciples, Asanga and Nagarjuna.

41 Je Tsongkapa, *Lam rim bsdus don ma (Lamrim Döndunma):*
    bstan pa tham cad 'gal med rtoks pa dang/gsung rab ma lus gdams
    par char wa dang/rgyal ba'i dgongs pa bde blag rnyed pa dang/nye
    spyod chen po'i gyang sa las kyang bsrung.

42 Verse 6 of the Water Shastra.

43 At a relative level, Sangha are a community of ordained monks
    or nuns. At an ultimate level, Sangha are those Bodhisattvas
    who have attained the path of seeing and beyond.

44 Buddhahood is a state in which one has completely abandoned
    the mental afflictions and the obstacles to omniscience, in
    which compassion, wisdom and spiritual powers are perfected.
    For a more detailed description, see *Liberation in Our Hands,*
    by *skyab rje pha bong kha pa rin po che byams pa stan 'dzin*
    'phrin las rgya mtso, 3 Vols. English translation, Sermey
    Khensur Lobsang Tharchin with Artemus B. Engle, New
    Jersey: Mahayana Sutra and Tantra Press, 1990-2001.

45 Je Tsongkapa, *Lam rim bsdus don ma: 'di phyi'i legs tshogs ji*
    snyed pa'i/rten 'brel legs par 'grig pa'i rtsa ba ni/lam ston bshes
    gnyen dam pa 'bad pa yis/bsam dang sbyor bas tshul bzhin bsten
    pa ru/mthong nas srog gi phyir yang mi gtong bar/bka' bzhin sgrub
    pa'i mchod pas mnyes par bya/rnal 'byor ngas. kyang nyams len de
    ltar byas/thar 'dod khyed kyang de bzhin bskyang 'tshal lo.

46 Such births are termed "lower" due to the intensity of the
    suffering experienced.

47 *Samsara:* the cycle of birth and death driven by our mental
    afflictions and karma.

48 Verse 51 of the Water Shastra.

49 Verses three and four of the Wood Shastra.

50 *Essence of Nectar* (Tib: *bdud vtsi snying po*) by Yeshe Tsondru,
    translated by Geshe Lobsang Tharchin with Benjamin and
    Deborah Alterman. Library of Tibetan Works & Archives,
    Dharamsala, India, 1979.

51 Verse eight of the Wood Shastra.

52 From Dipamkara Atisha's (Tib: *mar me mdzad a ti sha*) *Lamp of the Path to Enlightenment* (Tib: *byang chub lam gyi sgron ma*): *gang zhig thab ni gang dag gis/'khor ba'i bde ba tsam dag la/rang nyid don du gnyer byed pa/de ni skyes but tha mar shes.*

53 Nihilistic views include such assumptions as doubting that past and future lives exist, denying that actions lead to effects (i.e., rejecting the law of karma), and thinking that there is no such thing as enlightenment. Eternalistic views include such notions as thinking one's current conditions and future conditions are due to fate, holding to the view that there is an eternal/ unchanging soul, and so forth.

54 From *The Middle Length Discourses of the Buddha* translated by Bhikkhu Nanamoli and Bhikkhu Bodhi, Wisdom Publications, Boston, 1995, pages 506-519.

55 When used in this context, the word *dharma* refers to mundane phenomena.

56 Kadampa Geshes (*ka gdams pa dge shes*) were followers of Master Atisha (982-1054) and his lay disciple Dromtonpa (Tib: *'brom ston pa*, 1005-1064), who were renowned for the purity and austerity of their practice as well as for their scholarship and strict adherence to the teachings.

57 *Vajra* has many meanings, especially in the context of the secret teachings of Buddhism, but here it primarily connotes indestructibility and inseparability.

58 Verse 95 of the Water Shastra.

59 This was said during a teaching by the late Sermey Khensur Lobsang Tharchin (Tib: *ser smad blo bzang thar phyin*) as he was adapting a similar comment made to him by one of his teachers.

60 Ibid. Verse 101.

61 The path of seeing is the third of five increasingly refined levels of insight into the ultimate nature of reality. At the path of seeing, the practitioner experiences a direct, non-conceptual view of emptiness of self nature within a state of calm-abiding (shamatha).

62 Verse 104 of the Water Shastra.

63 Verse 16 of the Wood Shastra.

64 These are seven of the ten concordant results. The remaining three are: adultery resulting in having an unfaithful spouse, lying resulting in being slandered and deceived, and divisiveness leading to loss of friendships.

65 These include the five precepts for laypeople (to avoid killing, stealing, sexual misconduct, lying and intoxication) as well as the more numerous vows for the various levels of monks and nuns.

66 From Dipamkara Atisha's *Lamp of the Path to Enlightenment*: *srid pa'i bde la rgyab phogs shing/sdig pa'i las las ldog bdag nyid/ gang zhig rang zhi tsam don gnyer/skyes bu de ni 'bring zhes bya.*

67 Je Tsongkapa, *Lam rim bsdus don ma: sdug bden nyes dmigs bsam la ma 'bad na/thar pa don gnyer ji bzhin mi skye zhing/kun 'byung 'khor ba'i 'jug rim ma bsams na/'khor wa'i rtsa bag cod tshul mi shes pas/srid las nges 'byung skyo shas bsten pa dang/'khor bar gang gis bcings pa shes pa gces/rnal 'byor ngas kyang nyams len de ltar byas/thar 'dod khyed kyang de bzhin bskyang 'tshal lo.*

68 Verse 109 of the Water Shastra.

69 Quoted by Je Tsongkapa in *The Great Treatise on the Stages of the Path to Enlightenment,* translated by The Lamrim Chenmo Translation Committee, Joshua W.C. Cutler, Editor-In-Chief, Snow Lion Publications, Ithaca, New York, 2000. Volume One, page 298.

70 Ibid. Page 300.

71   It is said that meditative absorption free from craving and hankering for meditative bliss can create a type of karma that leads to rebirth into the fourth level of the form realm or into one of the four levels of the formless realm. However, these high states of existence are still within the cycle of birth and death.

72   "Stained impulse" refers to directing thoughts that are stained by their association with the first link, ignorance.

73   This quote accompanies the Buddha's depiction of the Wheel of Life: *steng du brtsam par bya zhing dbyung bar bya/sangs rgyas bstan la 'jug par bya/'dam bu'i khyim du glang chen bzhin/'chi bdag sde ni gzhom par bya. Gang zhig rab tu bag yod pas/chos 'dul 'di la spyod 'gyur ba/skye ba'i 'khor ba rab spang nas/sdug bsngal tha mar byed par 'gyur.*

74   Verse 21 of the Wood Shastra.

75   From Dipamkara Atisha's *Lamp of the Path to Enlightenment*: *rang rgyud gtoks pa'i sdug bsngal gyis/gang zhig gzhan gyi sdug bsngal kun/yang dag zad par kun nas 'dod/skes bu de ni mchog yin no.*

76   *Bodhicitta* is the intent to seek enlightenment in order to benefit all sentient beings.

77   The Great Vehicle (Sanskrit: *Mahayana*) derives its name from the vastness of its goal: the liberation of all sentient beings.

78   From *Samyutta Nikaya,* Pali, Vol. One, translated by Nyanaponika Thera, Buddhist Publication Society, Ceylon. Another translation by Bhikkhu Bodhi can be found in *The Connected Discourses of the Buddha* Volume One, Wisdom Publications, 2000.

79   Verse 112 of the Water Shastra.

80   Chapter 8, Verse 155, *Engaging in Bodhisattva Activities.* The translation used here was drawn from *Achieving Bodhicitta* by

Sermey Kensur Lobsang Tharchin, Mahayana Sutra and Tantra Press, Howell, New Jersey, 1999.

81   "The awakened ones" refers to the Buddhas.

82   *Engaging in Bodhisattva Activities*, Chapter 8, Verse 129.

83   Verse 24 of the Wood Shastra.

84   Je Tsongkapa, *Lam rim bsdus don ma: sbyin pa 'gro ba'i re skong yid bzhin nor/ser sna'i mdud pa gcod pa'i mtshon cha mchog/ma zhum snying stobs bskyed pa'i rgyal sras spyod/snyan pa'i grag pa phyogs bcur sgrog pa'i gzhi/de ltar shes nas lus dang long spyod dge/ yongs su gtong ba'i lam bzang mkhas pa bsten//rnal 'byor ngas kyang nyams len de ltar byas/thar 'dod khyed kyang de bzhin bskyang 'tshal lo.*

85   Verse 116 of the Water Shastra.

86   Je Tsongkapa, *Lam rim bsdus don ma: tsul khrims nyes spyod dri ma 'khrud pa'i chu/nyon mongs tsha gdung sel ba'i zla ba'i 'od/skke dgu'i dbus na lhun po lta bur brjid/stobs kyis bsdigs pa med par 'gro kun 'dud.*

87   Shantideva, *A Guide to the Bodhisattva's Way of Life*, translated by Stephen Batchelor, Library of Tibetan Works and Archives, Dharamsala, 1979.

88   Verse 27 of the Wood Shastra.

89   Verse 119 of the Water Shastra.

90   Je Tsongkapa, *Lam rim bsdus don ma: bsam gtan sems la dbang bsgyur rgyal po ste/bzhag na gyo med ri yi dbang po bzhin/btang na dge ba'i dmigs pa kun l 'jug/lus sems las su rung ba'i bde chen 'dren.*

91   Ibid. *shes rab zab mo'i de nyid lta wa'i mig/srid pa'i rtsa bad rungs nas 'byin pa'i lam/gsung rab kun las bsngags pa'i yon tan gter/gti mug mun sel sgron me mchog tug rags.*

92   Verse 120 of the Water Shastra.

93   Ibid. Verse 124.

94   Ibid. Verse 125.

95   From Lama Chopa (Tib: *bla ma mchod pa*) composed by *blo bzang chos kyi rgyal mthsan: phyi nang chos rnams sgyu ma rmi lam dang/dvangs ba'i mtsho nang zla gzugs ji bzhin du/snang yang bden par med pa'i tshul rtogs nas/ sgyu ma'i ting 'dzin rdzogs par byin gyis rlobs; 'khor 'das rang bzhin rdul tsam med pa dang/ rgyu 'bras rten 'brel bslu ba med pa gnyis/phan tshun 'gal med grogs su 'char ba yi/klu sgrub dgongs don rtogs par byin gyis rlobs.*

96   Ibid. Verse 128.

97   The author uses the Tibetan word ting (Tib: *gting*, depth) to refer to Buddha's teachings on profound emptiness and ta (Tib: *mtha*, border, boundary or edge, rendered here poetically as "horizon") to connote vastness, referring to Buddha's teachings on relative phenomena and Bodhisattva activities.

98   According to Akya Yongdzin's commentary, Mare-Faced Mountain (Tib: *rgod ma kha*) is the name of the legendary Fiery Horse-Faced (peak) in the quarter of the Iron Mountains. It is volcanic, and is one of the peripheral Iron Mountains at the world's edge, rising out of the sea, its shape resembling a horse's head. Because of its volcanic blaze, it is called Horse-Face Fire and Fire of the Mare-Face Mouth. It is fabled to evaporate the surrounding ocean.

99   Ibid. Nadra (Tib: *Na kra*) is the name of a great sea monster.

100   Ibid. There is a legend that can be found in the 22nd chapter of the extensive life stories of the Buddha (Jataka), in which the Buddha and Ananda had previously both taken birth as chiefs of geese. They were staying in an isolated place at a lake that was exceptionally beautiful. Varanasi's King Sudhodana heard of their magnificent qualities and ordered the construction of a very attractive lake as a way to capture them and a trap was placed in the lake. At the urgent entreating of another flock of

geese, the two Bodhisattva leaders of the geese went to that lake where they were caught in its trap.

101   Thin-eared (Tib: *rna ba srab pa*) is a colloquial term that connotes being gullible.

102   Akya Yongdzin refers to a fable of a rabbit who once went to the shore of Lake Madrupa. A ripened fruit fell from the Dzambu tree making a splashing sound like "chel" (Tib: *cal*). The frightened rabbit was extremely startled. He said "Chel is coming" and ran away. On the way, he encountered a fox, a wolf, a bear, a yeti and many other predatory and large game animals. To all he cried "Chel is coming." Without understanding the cause of his fear, they too became frightened and ran away. They encountered a lion who demanded "What is this so-called 'Chel'?" "We don't know what it is," they responded. The questioning finally reached the rabbit, who led them to the shore of the lake and showed them. The lion said, "Don't be afraid, it was just the splashing sound of a falling fruit." All sighed with relief. The meaning of this fable is that, whatever issues may come, you must analyze them for yourself rather than just following what others think.

103   Ibid. This is a reference to a Vedic legend about the great deity Ishvara (Shiva) and his two queens, Uma and Ganga. It tells of how the goddess Ganga, taking the form of a river, descended into the human realm beginning from above Mount Kailash, where she landed and split into seven parts. The sound she made as she passed through an opening in the snow mountain displayed her in an alluring manner as she traveled into a great lake. A Siddha named Dzahu was abiding in the snow mountain's gorges at that time. Ganga's sound disturbed his concentration, which angered Siddha Dzahu, so he drank her in a single gulp. King Kelden Shingta (Bhagiratha) supplicated

Siddha Dzahu, who then regurgitated her. Therefore, the Ganga (i.e. the Ganges river) is also called Dzahu's daughter.

A more extensive account tells of how once there was a leader named Evil King, whose 60,000 sons died and were reborn in hell. Five generations later, his successor, King Kalden Shingta, wished to release his ancestors, Evil King's sons, from hell by means of getting Ganga to descend. Therefore, he pleased Bhrama by his strong practice of austerities. Because of that, Bhrama ordered Ganga to descend to the human realm, but Ganga did not want to go. Therefore, great Ishvara said, "Why won't you listen to your ancestor's command?" Whereupon he took up Ganga and placed her in the locks of his hair. Although she wanted to escape and circled in search for an exit for 100,000 years, she couldn't find the end of Ishvara's locks. Therefore, again King Kalden Shingta pleased great Ishvara, who responded by squeezing his locks. One drop fell out above Mount Kailash, which instantaneously became a great lake. That then became the seven rivers: the Sita, Sidhu, Pa, Ganga, Kel, Tsimpa, and Nali. Ganga went through the snow mountain to the earth below. When she reached hell, the remaining karma of Evil King's 60,000 sons was washed pure. Therefore, they passed away from hell and were reborn in higher realms.

The stories of Evil King's 60,000 sons and Vishnu's 10 forms are included in Lobpon Sherab Gocha's "Commentary to the Exceptionally Superior Praises" and in Lhalay Puljung's "Extensive Commentary to the Praises."

104   Ibid. Once, a blind turtle was dwelling in a well. One day an ocean wave washed up another turtle, who traveled to the well. The blind turtle showed him a corner of his well and asked the sea turtle, "Is your ocean as big as this?" The sea turtle answered, "It's bigger than that." So, the blind turtle showed

him a little more of the well and asked, "Is it bigger than this?" The sea turtle said, "Even bigger than that." Eventually, the blind turtle asked, "Is the ocean as large as half of the well?" The sea turtle became displeased and said, "You are ignorant and blind. You know nothing. The great ocean's depth and expanse are extremely difficult to fathom. Therefore, how can you compare it to the well?" The blind turtle had praised only his dwelling, having thought "nothing else exists but this well of mine." Therefore, he was shocked.

105 Ibid. "Liquid rock," Doshun (Tib: *rdo zhun*), is a kind of pitch derived from burning a type of white rock or white dirt (mineral) in fire. When cool water is poured on it and stirred, it causes heat to rise and then causes the water to boil. [This may be a reference to lye or something similar.]

106 Ibid. "Cooking mantra," may be what's called "the boiling mantra," a prayer which when recited over water is said to instantly cool the water.

107 Ibid. This is a reference to a Vedic fable which tells of a Siddha named Bikshata who became overwhelmed with grief at the death of his son. Tying a vajra around his waste, he jumped into the Sita River. The river became so frightened; it split into a hundred branches.

108 Ibid. It is said that when geese go to eat lotus roots in the water, they become frightened if the moon's image is reflected. Afterward, even during the daytime, they remain frightened that the moon's image is still in the water and thus are unable to eat the lotus roots.

109 This is a play on words that the author is using to make his point. In Tibetan, a lotus (Tib: *pad ma*) is also known as "water-born" (Tib: *chu skye*).

110 This is a reference to young children identified soon after birth as reincarnations of previous great teachers (Tib: *sprul sku*).

The author is chastising those who have been misidentified, or who then go on to become arrogant or rely merely on their reputation.

111   Akya Yongdzin refers here to a fable about a rabbit and a lion who were accompanying each other. The lion bullied the rabbit many times making the rabbit become resentful and develop the wish to kill the lion. One time, the rabbit saw a deep well filled with water. He said to the lion, "Down in the well is an adversary who wants to fight you." Growing proud, the lion went to the edge of the well and looked down. He saw his reflection, and thought it to be his opponent. When he showed many expressions, the reflection in the water also showed exactly the same expressions. This angered the lion, who jumped into the well and died.

112   This is an ancient formula describing the formation of a world system.

113   This is an ancient description of an aspect of this world system.

114   Akya Yongdzin notes that this is a wheel with many buckets bound to it, which draws water up from a low-lying place.

115   Akya Yongdzin's commentary states that "In the valley of worldly Brahma's locks" and so forth seems to refer to the myth in the verse above with the account of King Kelden Shingta (Bhagiratha) and the descent of the Ganges, when saying "in the valley of the great worldly god's locks." Moreover, it appears that the terms "the great god Ishvara" and "Holder of the Ganges" are synonymous.

116   These are the obstacles of the mental afflictions (preventing liberation) and the obstacles pertaining to wisdom (preventing omniscience).

117   According to Akya Yongdzin's commentary, the seven kinds of water, based on a medical treatise, are: 1) water from rain, 2) water from snow, 3) water from a valley, 4) spring water, 5)

well water, 6) sea water, and 7) water from trees. In order, the first is superior and the ones following are of lesser and lesser quality.

118   "The Victor's speech" means the Buddha's teachings.

119   Akya Yongdzin says that "descending in stages, come the three paths" refers to the Ganges. It is said to flow in three paths or to descend in three paths because it travels through, or descends through, the three (realms) of the higher state (of celestial life), the region of humans, and below the earth (lower realms of existence).

120   Ibid. In the passage with the words "the water offering to the fortunate one, Completely Awakened," the namsay (Tib: *rnam sad*), a Tibetan word that literally means "awake" is a term for a god. Gods are called this because they ordinarily go without sleep. The gods made a water offering of the Ganges to the feet of Vishnu, in joy over his defeat of the asuras. Because of this, the Ganges is called "the Deva's water offering to the feet of Vishnu (Skt: *Vishnupada*)." "The One Who Is Awake" is a name generally given to a god, but here it is to be understood as applying specifically to Vishnu.

121   "Lama Manjugosha" is a reference to Je Tsongkapa.

122   Akya Yongdzin's commentary states that the line, "the four Vedas sinking in the ocean" refers to Vishnu in a fish's form drawing the Vedas from the water. In Vedic accounts, it is related that Vishnu has ten avatars: 1) a fish, 2) a tortoise, 3) a boar, 4) Lion Man, 5) a dwarf, 6) Joyous One (a hero), 7) Rama, 8) Krishna, 9) the Buddha, and 10) Karaka (Karki). Having emanated himself in the form of a fish, Vishnu drew the Vedas which were sinking below the surface of the ocean. The four classes of Vedas are: 1) hymns/poetry, 2) authoritative speech, 3) offering rites, and 4) works, intended for the protection of life.

123   Ibid. The lines "all the earth's trees, leaves and fruit/ are the kindness of the naga dwelling in Lake Madru," refers to the legend that if the Naga King were not in Lake Madru, Lake Madru would not come to be, without which, there would be no cause for the earth's waters. Therefore, the trees and so forth would not arise. Not only that, but it says in the *Sutrasamuccaya* that the world's abundance and all its enjoyments, as well as the jewels of the ocean depend on the power of Lake Madrupa.

124   Empty animal skin bags called tong kyal (Tib: *stong rkyal*) were used by Tibetans as life preservers and for learning how to swim.

125   "General meanings" has been used here to translate the technical term tra chi (Tib: *sgra spyi*), which refers to the images of a subject in one's mind that one has heard about but not yet experienced directly. In this case, it refers to one who is listening to teachings on Dharma, thinking about them, and eventually, meditating upon them in order to gain a direct experience of their truth.

126   The six types of birth are to be born as a denizen in hell, as a hungry ghost, as an animal, as a human, as a demigod, or as a god.

127   The eight types of leisure are: 1) not being in hell, 2) not being a hungry ghost, 3) not being an animal, 4) not being a long-lived worldly deity, 5) not being born in a region with no Dharma, 6) not being born in an era of no Dharma, 7) not being an imbecile/mute, and 8) not holding wrong views. Akya Yongdzin says the eight qualities of water are: 1) coolness, 2) sweetness, 3) lightness, 4) softness, 5) clarity, 6) being without pollution, 7) not causing illness in the throat, and 8) not causing illness in the stomach.

128   The three doors are the avenues of action by body, speech, and mind.

129   Akya Yongdzin comments: "Mountain peak" has the sense
       [in Sanskrit] of being at the verge of death. As it has been
       translated as "summit," (Tib: *rtse*) or "peak" (Tib: *zom bu*),
       [here it is] rendered as "mountain peak."

130   The three gems are the Buddha, Dharma and Sangha.

131   It is said that a god sees water as nectar, a human sees it as
       water, a hungry ghost perceives it as filth, and a hell-being
       sees it as molten lava. This is due to their varying karmic
       propensities.

132   The ocean.

133   The three trainings are the practices of morality, concentration
       and wisdom.

134   Akya Yongdzin describes a mythological episode involving the
       "pure naga" Rahu. This serpent lived in the ocean, and by the
       power of his presence there, a wave carried away a corpse so
       that it did not have any contact at all with his abode.

135   These three forms of compassion are: 1) perceiving sentient
       beings as the object of compassion while conceiving them as
       inherently existent (which is compared to the misperception of
       thinking a moon's reflection is a real moon abiding in water),
       2) compassion seeing the impermanence of sentient beings
       (compared to perceiving the wavering reflection of the moon),
       and 3) compassion seeing that beings are empty of self-nature
       (compared to seeing the unreality of a reflected moon).

136   A mythological tree on the southern continent, described in
       ancient Indian cosmology.

137   According to Akya Yongdzin, when the fabled fruit of the
       Jambu on Lake Madru is ripe, it falls into the lake. At that
       time, the nagas who live there, emanating themselves in the
       form of fish, eat the fruit. What is not consumed, by virtue
       of long contact with the lake's water, becomes the gold of the
       southern continent (Sanskrit: *Jambudvipa*).

138   According to Akya Yongdzin, the word ketaka means "to make clear." There are many ketakas: the ketaka jewel, the ketaka fruit tree, etc. In the instance of the ketaka tree, its fruit, when it falls into water, immediately clears away any sediment.

139   Ibid. *Bendurya*, when translated, is called "very clear jewel." Three kinds of this exist: white, yellow, and blue, each previous one said to be superior to the latter. Some also say there is a black type.

140   Ibid. The name Agastya corresponds to the Tibetan names for the constellation Canopus, ri shi (Tib: *ri byi*), also called ri dor (Tib: *ri 'dor*), literally, "mountain-abandonment," or ri phen (Tib: *ri 'phen*), literally, "mountain-throw." *A gas* means "non-moving," which is a term for a mountain. *Stya* can be taken either as "to forsake" or as "to throw," according to the explanation found in the commentary on the *Deathless Treasury* (a Sanskrit dictionary), called *The Wish-Fulfilling*. There, *rishi* is one term given for "heavenly sage," that is, one who possesses clairvoyance and magical powers.

At one time [according to legend], two demigods, brothers called Wind-Attainment and Earth-Possessor, were sending forth many emanations. Wind-Attainment emanated his own body as food, [and the two demigods] called the heavenly rishis to a feast. Induced to come, no sooner had the sages eaten the food than Earth-Possessor called [his brother's] name. At this, the rishis' stomachs were ripped open and Wind-Attainment emerged. Through such means, many divine sages were murdered.

At another occasion, when [the demigod brothers again] called some rishis to a feast and were going to act as they had before, one of the rishis, by the strength of his magical abilities, [ate] Wind-Attainment and digested him. By virtue of this, the rishi become very thirsty and drank in one gulp all the oceans and sources of moisture. Afterward, he engendered compassion for all the beings living in the water. Regurgitating it, he made this prayer: "May the water I drank become endowed with the eight [good] qualities." By the power of his aspiration, it became nectar possessing those eight qualities.

141   Thusness (Tib: *de nyid*) is the emptiness of self-existence.

142   The four ways of gathering disciples are to give them material aid, encouragement, and Dharma teachings, and then to practice the Dharma in accord with what has been taught.

143   Akya Yongdzin's commentary explains that in the practice of certain rituals entailing a water pitcher, the mantra *Om tapte, tapte, mahatapte, svaha* is uttered. When translated, *Om* is the leader of the mantra. *Tapte* could be taken as "suffering mother," "sweltering mother," or "hot mother." Here, *tapte* is translated as "suffering mother," and it is an invocation. When the invocation is made to the "suffering mother," it is synonymous with the name of the divine river Ganges; according to received explanation, that is what is being called upon. The mantra when it is translated is "Om suffering mother, great suffering mother, so be it." When the mantra is pronounced, through having called on the name of the Ganges and summoned it, one imagines that the water in the vase turns into milk.

144   Ibid. "The abode of the naga king" is a term for the ocean. The Tibetan idiom deng chen (*gdengs can*) is a synonym for naga. The lord of such beings is the Nagaraja; the realm of the Nagaraja is the ocean.

145   Ibid. The four empowerments are: 1) the vase empowerment, 2) the secret empowerment, 3) the wisdom empowerment, and the 4) word empowerment.

146   Ibid. The two types of attainments are the common and supreme attainments. Common attainments include various supernormal abilities and the supreme attainment is the non-dual state of Vajradhara.

147   Ibid. The knowledge of thusness is obtained via knowledge of the true nature of the objects of sensual desire.

148   Tibetans will hold a burn near fire to soothe it.

149   There are two stages of practice in Buddhist Tantra. This is a reference to the first and the following verse refers to the second.

150   The story of this king is told in the *Ramayana*. In brief, Kelden Shingta (Bhagiratha) performed austerities to obtain a boon from Brahma. Pleased with his efforts the god asked the king what he desired. Bhagiratha replied that he wanted Brahma to let the sacred river Ganges descend to earth so that he could perform funerary rites for his ancestors, to expiate their sins and release their spirits to paradise. The god complied, and with the aid of Shiva, who broke the onrush of the river's otherwise cataclysmic fall, let the Ganges flow to the terrestrial realm.

151   According to Akya Yongdzin's commentary, the four types of joy are: 1) joy, 2) supreme joy, 3) exceptional joy, and 4) simultaneously born joy.

152   Ibid. The four types of emptiness are: 1) empty, 2) extremely empty, 3) greatly empty, and 4) completely empty.

153   Ibid. The four rivers are: 1) the Ganges, 2) the Sindhu, 3) the Pakshu, and 4) the Sita.

154   See endnote to verse 20 of the Water Shastra for a description of Mare-faced Mountain, though in this case the author is using the analogy to refer to the secret yoga of inner heat.

155   Wind-mind (Tib: *rlung sems*) is a technical term used in Highest Yoga Tantra to describe the most subtle continuum of mind that travels from life to life.

156 The energy center (Skt: *chakra*) at the throat is known as the enjoyment *chakra*.

157 The three bodies are a Buddha's *Dharmakaya, Sambhogakaya,* and *Nirmanakaya.*

158 The author is referring here to taking full refuge in the Buddha, Dharma and Sangha.

159 "Lesser peace" refers to individual Nirvana, which is the goal of Hearers and Solitary Realizers, as opposed to the full state of enlightenment sought by Bodhisattvas in order to accomplish the welfare of all beings.

160 Akya Yongdzin comments: The Tala tree, as it is called in India at this time, has leaves which can be fashioned into a sort of writing paper or also into a fan, and so forth.

161 Ibid. Concerning the Nyadrota tree, it is said that the Tibetan names *nya gro tha, bhu bad,* and *pa ta* are synonymous. In Tibetan language it is called Kang mang (*rkang mang*), literally, "many feet" or many units of measure, so-named because the seeds of the Nyadrota are just a quarter of the size of a white mustard seed, but it is said that each year, its branches grow to cover the distance traveled by the sound of a yell, increasing and developing to an extremely great extent.

162 The peak of samsara is the most refined level of meditation in the formless realm. Having reached this lofty state, one can still fall back into lower states of existence.

163 Akya Yongdzin explains that the tikta is a root with a very bitter taste. Nowadays it is thought that an extract of it can be made into a medicine that has the ability to heal feverous sickness.

164 The three superior trainings are morality, concentration and wisdom.

165 Akya Yongdzin says that, concerning the Dzendu's seeds (Tib: *dzan du*), Dzendu is the name of the *Udamwara.* The

Udamwara is called "the demon's conqueror." Its exceptional flower that came to being and blossomed at the time Buddha came into the world with a bloom the size of a chariot wheel and a scent that covered 4,000 fathoms. It is extremely rare and is described in such texts as *A Hundred Stanzas Elucidating How to Achieve Realizations* and so forth.

166   Shravakas (Hearers) and Pratyekabuddhas (Solitary Realizers) gain liberation for themselves by eliminating their mental afflictions, but they lack the *bodhicitta* motivation, which thus renders them less capable than a Bodhisattva.

167   Akya Yongdzin remarks that the Wish-Granting Tree (Tib: *dpags bsam shing*) is called the *kawatrika*. It is said to exist in the place of the gods and is able to bestow all temporal needs and desires.

168   Definite goodness refers to liberated states in which there is no more return to states of suffering.

169   Haribadra, in his commentary to Maitreya's *Ornament of Clear Realization* entitled *Light for the Ornament of Clear Realization,* mentions eleven types of clairvoyance. The "five eyes" are: 1) the "fleshy eye" which sees the specifics of distant objects, 2) the "divine eye" which can see when someone will die and where they will be reborn, 3) the "wisdom eye" which directly sees that phenomena are empty of self-nature, 4) the "Dharma eye" which can perceive the level of realization of Arya beings, and 5) the "Buddha eye" which can thoroughly perceive all aspects of every phenomena in a single instant. He also mentions six direct super-knowledges: 1) the power of performing miracles, 2) supernormal hearing, 3) reading the thoughts of others, 4) recollection of the previous lives of oneself and others, 5) the ability to see all forms, and 6) the elimination of mental afflictions. These clairvoyances are

obtained by Bodhisattvas practicing the six perfections as they develop meditative absorption (Tib: *bsam gtan*).

170   The three poisons are ignorance, hatred and desire.

171   Akya Yongdzin remarks that *bendurya*, when translated, is called "very clear jewel." Three kinds of this exist: white, yellow, and blue, each previous one said to be superior to the latter. Some also say there is a black type.

172   Ibid. Kye gu (Tib: *skye dgu*), translated here as "every kind of being," literally translates as "nine births," is taught in the *Dar* commentary of the *Jewel Rosary* (composed by Gyaltsab Dharma Rinchen) as referring to the five aggregates together with the four elements. These nine phenomena are the basis for labeling a being thus being called "nine births." According to Penchen Losang Chokyi Gyeltsan (*Pan chen blo bzang chos kyi rgyal mtshan*) the name derives from dying in the desire realm, and from there, transferring into the desire realm, into the form realm, or into the formless realm constituting three types of birth. Similarly, dying in both the form and formless realms and joining any of those three realms in the next birth makes nine possibilities, thus the term "nine births." Some say that the word *dgu* is not a count of nine, but should be spelled *skye rgu*, (with the head letter 'ra'). When described that way it means "many" (as in "many births").

173   Ibid. Malayar kye (Tib: *Malayar skye*), "Malaya born," is a general name for sandalwood, a term taken from a place name, that is, sandalwood born from Mount Malaya.

174   Akya Yongdzin comments that agar (Tib: *a gar*), translated here as Agarwood, is a name for *a ga ru*. Agarwood is resinous heartwood formed when Aquilana trees become darkened by a particular type of mold creating a fragrant resin called gaharu, jinko, agarwood, or oud. It is used for incense and perfumes in many cultures.

175   The Tibetan words chok tar (Tib: *phyogs mthar*), rendered here as "the ends of the world," appears to be a play on words because the phrase can also mean extreme views.

176   Ngen (Tib: *ngan*), rendered here as bad mark (connoting a bad situation, reputation and so forth), can also mean excrement, an apparent play on words given the image of the bird feces (*bya thal*).

177   According to Akya Yongdzin, *Sahaka'ra* is called "Simultaneously-born" in Tibetan. Some lexicons explain that it is the name for an exceptional type of mango made by pouring milk on the trunk of a mango tree. An especially superior type of fragrant mango fruit comes from plants nurtured in this way.

178   Lo dang denpa (Tib: *blo dang ldan pa*), translated here as "intelligence," appears to be a play on words because its literal meaning is "having mind."

179   According to Akya Yongdzin, "The flower of the sorrowless tree is not opened by the sun and moon. It is opened by the touch of a young woman's anklet." The sorrowless tree is called the *ashingka*. It is said that if one is unable to open its flower by the light of the sun and moon, then if it is touched by a young woman's ankle, it blooms. Concerning this, there is a legend that the great Ishvara put aside desire for his wife and practiced austerities in front of a tree, which fulfilled the goddess Gauri's aspiration. Thus, the tree was named "sorrowless."

180   Akya Yongdzin notes that the great ocean of the world is known as the "milk ocean." Though the author is not clear about whose throat he refers to here, given that his next verse is in honor of the Sakya Pandita, it is most likely a reference to him.

181 Ibid. Ngangmo (Tib: *ngang mo*) means swans. These Saraswati swans are analogies for the use of poetic ornamental imagery (explained in the second chapter of the text on poetry concerning analogies to forms).

182 Ibid. Yangden (Tib: *dbyangs ldan*), translated here as "poetry," refers to Sarasvati (the goddess of poetry).

183 Ibid. Dzinma (Tib: *'dzin ma*) is the name for the ground/earth. *Pandita*, when translated from Sanskrit, means scholar and also *Vedantin*.

184 Ibid. Kyi kang shepa (Tib: *mkhyid gang zhes pa*) is the name of the width of a fist combined with an extended thumb. Seven finger widths with an additional mid-joint length of a thumb is called a tshon (*mtshon*), which means "two fingers" or a "forefinger." This is explained in the chapter of the medicinal text dealing with demarcations on the upper part of the body.

185 Ibid. Dashel (Tib: *zla shel*) means water glass and can refer to both a jewel water glass and to the sphere of the moon. In this case it connotes the sphere of the moon (often used as a symbol of enlightenment).

186 In the West we think of the moon as having an image of a man's face whereas, in Tibet, they imagined it having the image of a rabbit.

About the Author

The Third Gungthang Rinpoche, Venerable Konchok Tenpai Dronme (1762–1823) was highly esteemed in Tibet as a great scholar and Buddhist practitioner. He revitalized Buddhism in Tibet and inspired many generations that followed. His written works are cherished by Tibetans and several translations of his works have been published around the world.

About the Translators

Yeshe Khedrup, the chief translator for this edition, currently works for Voice of America. At the age of 8 he was enrolled in the Lhasa Preparatory School in Tibet, and then from 15 until 19, studied at Drepung Monastery in Tibet. After escaping China's invasion, he resumed his studies in India from 1959-1963 at the Buxador re-settlement camp. He then entered teacher training and taught from 1965-1967 at the Mussoorie Tibetan School before coming to the United States.

Wilson Hurley, co-translator, has studied Tibetan Buddhism for over 30 years and serves as a lay teacher in the Washington DC area (www.mstcdharma.org). Professionally, he serves the community as a psychotherapist with an emphasis on the use of mindfulness for mental health. He has given meditation instructions, workshops and talks to several community and church groups.